TEACHING FOR SUCCESS

TEACHER'S TOOLKIT SERIES

1

Teaching for Success:
Developing Your Teacher Identity in Today's Classroom
Brad Olsen (UC–Santa Cruz)

2

Teaching English Learners:
Fostering Language and the Democratic Experience
Kip Téllez (UC–Santa Cruz)

3

Teaching Without Bells: What We Can Learn
from Powerful Practice in Small Schools
Joey Feldman (New Haven Unified School District)

4

Leading from the Inside Out:
Expanded Roles for Teachers in Equitable Schools
W. Norton Grubb and Lynda Tredway
(UC–Berkeley)

5

Teaching Toward Democracy:
Educators as Agents of Change
William Ayers (U of Ill–Chicago), Kevin Kumashiro (U of Ill–Chicago),
Erica Meiners (Northeastern Illinois University),
Therese Quinn (The Art Institute of Chicago), and David Stovall (U of Ill–Chicago)

6

Making a Difference:
Developing Meaningful Careers in Education
Karen Hunter Quartz (UCLA), Brad Olsen (UC–Santa Cruz),
Lauren Anderson (UCLA), and Kimberly Barraza Lyons (UCLA)

TEACHING FOR SUCCESS

Developing Your Teacher

Identity in Today's Classroom

Brad Olsen

TEACHER'S TOOLKIT SERIES

Paradigm Publishers
Boulder · London

Copyright © 2010 Paradigm Publishers

Published in the United States by Paradigm Publishers, 2845 Wilderness Place, Suite 200, Boulder, CO 80301 USA.

Paradigm Publishers is the trade name of Birkenkamp & Company, LLC, Dean Birkenkamp, President and Publisher.

Library of Congress cataloging-in-publication data is available at the Library of Congress.

ISBN 978-1-59451-868-3 (paperback : alk. paper)

Printed and bound in the United States of America on acid-free paper that meets the standards of the American National Standard for Permanence of Paper for Printed Library Materials.

Designed by Cindy Young.
Typeset by Mulberry Tree Enterprises.

13 12 11 10   1 2 3 4 5

CONTENTS

FOREWORD

FEW BOOKS IN THE FIELD of education have compelled me to keep turning the pages to find out what lies ahead while simultaneously creating a yearning in me to turn back the clock. This book is one of those few—a unique and intriguing combination of looking forward and reflecting backward at the same time. Yet I'm warning you, if you decide to begin turning the pages of this book, you should prepare yourself to be illuminated and frustrated at the same time. Why? Because as you begin reading, you might be asking yourself the same question that I did: *Where was this book when I really needed it as a beginning teacher twenty-five years ago?*

Just as this book is unique and compelling, so is the story of its author. I speak from direct experience after having first met Brad Olsen almost two decades ago in South America. At that time, he was a young but highly talented teacher who immediately connected with students from diverse backgrounds. Back then I was his building principal, and I watched him grow and develop as an educator with such dramatic speed that he quickly established himself as the "star teacher" on staff. Idealistic and passionate, Brad possessed a strong desire early in his career to keep asking the key questions: *What are teachers "supposed" to do? What defines a teacher? What does a "successful" classroom or school look like?* This yearning to understand the process of becoming a better teacher ultimately led Brad to pursue higher education and resulted in his subsequent research in the fields of teacher education and teacher identity. The critical questions that Brad asked himself then are the same ones that he ponders and probes in this book. Brad's combination of classroom experience and theoretical knowledge allows him to weave together research and practice in a way that makes for a gripping read.

How do you know if this book might be useful to you? From my perspective after working with educators across the entire teaching spectrum, from student teachers through master teachers, I believe that Brad Olsen's book provides multiple insights for everyone. Whether you are entering a teacher education program and worried primarily about preteaching concerns, a beginning teacher with day-to-day survival concerns, a more experienced teacher with classroom-situation concerns, or a master teacher with student-centered concerns, you will find yourself sharing a significant commonality with Brad and other readers: you are all in the process of becoming better teachers and learning to understand your unique *teacher identity*. As the author explains:

> The book introduces a model of teacher learning that illuminates how teachers . . . can systematically examine their own personal and professional teaching influences and work to adjust and assemble them in conjunction with education research into a coherent, successful whole. The result—that unique, successful whole—is what I call your teacher identity, and by better understanding it you will improve the kind of teacher you are in the classroom, the kind of learning you can offer your students, and the professional satisfaction you receive from your career.

If we believe in the maxim that knowledge is power, then we need to realize that our own self-knowledge as educators can serve as a powerful tool in day-to-day teaching and learning. Without this knowledge of yourself and your unique teacher identity, you place at significant risk your ability to maximize student learning in your classroom.

Brad Olsen reminds us that we are not teaching a classroom full of our clones, but rather a complex group of students with unique needs and disparate ways of learning. By understanding the influences from the past that have helped to shape each of our own teacher identities, and that continue to shape our teacher identities today, we can move away from a narrow approach of teaching in which we unconsciously follow our natural tendencies. In other words, the more we know about ourselves and the influences that have shaped us, the better we can meet the needs of our students and, of equal importance, meet our own needs by finding greater professional satisfaction as educators.

The process of becoming a great teacher never stops. As you enter the pages of this book, you will soon see this notion become a reality through Brad Olsen's personal insights as an educator and through the eyes of Liz, a teacher whose experience may feel startlingly and eerily similar to your own. As educators, whether we are anticipating the approach of our first day as a teacher or entering our third decade in the classroom, we actually have far more in common than we might imagine. This book highlights our commonalities by deftly connecting theory and practice, helping us to understand and better manage the fact that, as Brad puts it, "multiple, often hidden, frequently personal influences on your own growth as a teacher are continually working to shape the educator you are—and are continually becoming." And I find it noteworthy that a "star teacher" whom I saw in action many years ago continues to believe it for himself: in this book he writes, "I still have work to do on the journey. Like all teachers, I'm still becoming."

If you keep turning these pages, I believe that you will find, as I have, that we can all learn lessons from a master teacher and leading researcher who still believes that becoming a teacher signifies a worthy quest, the pursuit of something significant that will bring value both to our own lives and to the lives of many others.

—Dr. Eric H. Habegger
International School Administrator
Colombia, Qatar, Japan, Venezuela, Paraguay

SERIES FOREWORD

THIS TEACHER'S TOOLKIT series is a set of six related books written for prospective, new, and experienced teachers who are committed to students and families, who conceive of themselves as agents of democratic change, and who are eager to think more deeply, more broadly, and more practically about their work in education. All six books succinctly link theory with practice, present extended arguments for improving education, and wrap their discussions around successful examples of the topics in question.

Although each book is its own resource, the books in the Toolkit series share some common views about teaching. For one, all of the books treat teachers not as mere deliverers of curriculum but as active, three-dimensional professionals capable of diagnosing student learning, developing powerful educational experiences, assessing and adjusting student learning, and forming productive relationships with children and adults in schools. Another view all of the books share is that teaching is hard work that is among the most important kinds of work any society requires. My grandmother used to say that no society can survive without farmers or teachers. I think that is still true. Teaching is undeniably difficult work, but it is also frequently enjoyable work because it is so challenging, meaningful, and success oriented. These books are for teachers who have accepted the challenges of teaching because they relish the satisfaction of the work, they enjoy helping young people grow, and they know that quality education is necessary for the health of our world.

A third commonality about teaching among these books is their shared presumption that teachers are always looking for ways to improve. Teaching is a profession in which one enters as a novice, develops expertise over time, and continues to grow and change throughout the whole of one's career. The Toolkit books are written for teachers at multiple points in their career cycle: Beginning teachers will learn new ways to think about learning, students, and what it means to become a successful educator. Early- and middle-career teachers can reflect on their own practice in light of the ideas, strategies, and stories of these books—and they can use the books to deepen and broaden their future work. Veteran teachers can see themselves and their varied experiences inside the perspectives of the books, as well as figure out how they can continue to challenge themselves and their students—and perhaps take on other kinds of education work such as mentoring newer teachers, advocating for students on a broader stage, or writing about their own teaching. No matter where readers are in their education careers, these books offer powerful learning and useful opportunities for professional reflection.

The six books are sequenced to loosely follow both the career cycle of teaching and the fact that, as teachers progress, they often widen their sphere of influence. Book 1 in the series is *Teaching for Success: Developing Your Teacher Identity in Today's Classroom* by Brad Olsen. This book focuses on the processes of "becoming a teacher" and explores how to teach well in this contemporary age. Wrapping its conversations about teacher development around the core concept of teacher identity, the book offers its own teacher learning experience: how to recognize, adjust, and maximize the many ways your personal self and your professional self become integrated in your teaching work.

Book 2, *Teaching English Learners: Fostering Language and the Democratic Experience*, by Kip Téllez, focuses on what teachers can do in their classrooms in order to better understand and more effectively teach English learners. Drawing from research and experience not only on learning and teaching but also on culture, language, immigration, and contemporary politics, Téllez offers a unique guide for use by U.S. teachers interested in deeply and compassionately supporting the growth of students whose native language is not English.

Book 3 in the series is *Teaching Without Bells: What We Can Learn from Powerful Instruction in Small Schools* by Joey Feldman. This book offers a valuable look at how teaching and learning are fundamentally influenced by school size. The book's premise is that student and teacher experiences in education are direct functions of their school's size (and its accompanying influence on how schools are organized). Focusing on challenges and benefits of teaching in small high schools, Feldman's book helps readers consider where they might want to teach and—no matter the size of their school site—how they can teach well by maximizing lessons from the small schools movement.

Book 4, *Leading from the Inside Out: Expanded Roles for Teachers in Equitable Schools*, by Norton Grubb and Lynda Tredway, opens up the professional world of the teacher by offering new ways to think about school reform from the vantage point of the teacher. The authors make a compelling case for teachers as the key ingredient in education reform and schools as the lever for democratic educational change. Presenting a blueprint for a new kind of school in which teachers are not only classroom instructors but education reformers as well, Grubb and Tredway illustrate why we have the schools we have today and how broad-minded teachers can transform them into successful schools for tomorrow.

Book 5, *Teaching Toward Democracy: Educators as Agents of Change*, by William Ayers, Kevin Kumashiro, Erica Meiners, Therese Quinn, and David Stovall, also considers teachers as agents of change on a broader scale. The authors share their ideas about how teachers can better humanize schooling for students, combat some of the current failings of market models of education, and extend their teaching work past the school day and outside the school walls. Their book invites readers into a view of education through the eyes of students, and it provides thoughtful strategies to enact teaching for social justice as not just a popular slogan but as an authentic focus on human rights and social equity for all.

And, to close out the series, Book 6, *Making a Difference: Developing Meaningful Careers in Education*, by Karen Hunter Quartz, Brad Olsen, Lauren Anderson, and Kimberly Barraza Lyons, looks at whole careers in education. This book examines the dynamic lives and work of several educators in Los Angeles and investigates why teachers stay in the classroom or shift to other kinds of education roles, such as school administrator, curriculum coordinator, or teacher mentor. The book unpacks the sometimes maddening complexity of the teaching profession and offers a roadmap for how teachers can, themselves, remain challenged and satisfied as educators without relaxing their commitments to students.

There are different approaches to reading the books in this series. One way is to consider the whole series as a coherent set of sequenced conversations about teaching. In this manner, you might read the books one at a time, all the way through, inserting yourself into the text of the books: Do the stories and experiences in the books ring true for you? How will you use these books to improve your practice, broaden your influence, and deepen your professional satisfaction? You might imagine, as you read the books this way, that you are sitting in a room with the authors—listening to their ideas, questioning them, actively engaging with their arguments, or talking back to the text when necessary.

Or perhaps you might use these books as textbooks—as thoughtful primers on selected topics that interest you. In this manner, you might pick and choose particular chapters to study: Which specific ideas will you implement in your teaching tomorrow? Are there further readings or key resources that you will hunt down and look at on your own? What concrete activities will you try out? Write notes in the margins of the books and return to the chapters regularly. Photocopy single pages (not whole chapters, please!) to share with peers. Use the books as you plan lessons or design curricula. Engage with the reflection questions at the end of each book's chapters. You will find occasionally in the margins cross-references on specific topics to other books in the series. When you read "Cross-Reference, See Book 2 ..." you can use the numbered list of titles on p. ii to correlate each reference to the intended book.

Or, you may pick some of the books to read collectively with other educators—maybe with your teacher education cohort, or as a group of teachers working with a mentor, or perhaps as part of a teacher inquiry group that you set up with colleagues. Group discussion of these books allows their arguments, perspectives, and examples to prompt your own collective reflection and professional growth: What themes from the books call out to you? What points might you disagree with? How might different educators among you interpret parts of these books in different, perhaps competing, ways? How can these books inspire you to create specific collaborative projects or teacher networks at your school site? You may find the reflection questions at the end of each chapter particularly useful for group conversation.

This series of books is called the "Teacher's Toolkit," but maybe, for some, the idea of a *toolkit* for teachers may not, at first glance, be apt. Picturing a toolkit could conjure images of a steel toolbox or superhero's belt full of hardware for educators—a diagnostic screwdriver, the clawhammer of homework, a set of precision wrenches for adjusting student learning on the fly. Such images are, well, just too instrumental. They risk suggesting that teaching is mechanical or automatic, or that what good educators do is select utensils from their box to apply when needed. That doesn't describe the kind of teaching I know and love. It erroneously suggests that students are to be fastened with bolts or hammered into obedience, or that learning is gut-wrenchingly rigid. And, to my mind, such a view treats teachers as technicians trained by rote, using tools given to them by others, following directions written on the outside of the box.

Instead, the authors of these books conceive of education as less fixed, more fluid, less finished, more uncertain, and certainly far more complicated than anything for which traditional tools would work. These authors—based on their own years of experience as classroom teachers, educational researchers, school administrators, and university professors—view education similarly to educational philosopher John Dewey when, in 1934, he wrote:

> About 40 years ago, a new idea dawned in education. Educators began to see that education should parallel life, that the school should reproduce the child's world. In this new type of education the child, instead of the curriculum, became the centre of interest, and since the child is active, changing, creative—education ceased to be static, [and] became dynamic and creative in response to the needs of the child.[1]

Like Dewey, I understand teaching and learning to be context-specific, highly creative, dynamically student-centered activities that are as complicated and multifaceted as life itself. And just as important.

So let's reimagine the analogy of a teacher's toolkit. A *toolkit* for teachers could instead be a metaphor for a thoughtful, useful, provocative bundle of perspectives, theories, and approaches for teachers—a set of lively teaching discussions written by different authors who share some common ground. This bundle would empathize with teachers since its authors are all teachers, as well as education researchers and writers: they know both how difficult and how rewarding teaching can be. But it would also exhort teachers not to fall down on the job—not to shirk their work, make excuses, or lessen their resolve to support students.

The bundle of teaching conversations could share stories from the classroom that reveal teaching to be kaleidoscopic: made up of thousands of shifting views, hundreds of competing relations, and dozens of different ways to succeed with children. The stories would reveal how to be a great teacher and why doing so is so damned important. The bundle of ideas and perspectives would include actual examples of good teaching, lesson ideas, and lots of research tidbits useful for prospective and practicing educators. Yes, that could be a toolkit I would want to own. It would be a kit full of thoughtful perspectives, research summaries, wisdom of practice, and impassioned words of advice from handpicked educationalists. An "idea kit," really. A boxed set of thoughtful primers on how to teach well for social change in the current global climate.

John Dewey famously built up binaries in his writing—teaching is either this or that; students learn in this way but not in that way—only to collapse the binary in the end and suggest that education is too complicated for easy contradictions. So I'll take a page from Dewey's playbook and attempt the same. Maybe we can consider this book series as not an either/or. Not as *either* a box of teaching instruments *or* a collection of thoughtful conversations about education, but as both: a set of tangible strategies for teachers to make their own and a loosely bundled collection of professional arguments for use by educators in order to think for themselves, but in deeper and newer ways than before. That's the way that I prefer to envision this teacher's toolkit.

No matter how you choose to make use of the books in the Teacher's Toolkit, it is our sincere hope that you will find value in them. We have tried to make them accessible, conversational, substantive, and succinct. We all believe that teaching is a fundamentally important profession, and, if this world is to improve and grow, it will be because our teachers can help future generations to become wise, creative, and critical thinkers who put their ideas into action toward improving the societies they will inherit. You are an essential part of that human process.

—Brad Olsen
University of California, Santa Cruz

NOTE

1. Dewey, J. 1934. "Tomorrow May Be Too Late: Save the Schools Now." Reprinted in J. Boydston (ed.), *John Dewey: The Later Works, 1925–1953: 1933–1934, Vol. 9* (Carbondale: Southern Illinois University Press, 1986), 386.

ACKNOWLEDGMENTS

I F I HAD WRITTEN THIS BOOK all by myself, it wouldn't be a very good book at all. If this book has value, that's only partly attributable to me. It's more likely a function of all that I've learned from my own teachers and students throughout the years—and from current colleagues and others who have supported me in my work. Particular thanks go out to Eric Habegger, Lauren Anderson, Judith Warren Little, Jeannie Oakes, and Dean Birkenkamp. Also, thanks to Dena Sexton for her help with parts of Chapter 5. And, of course, great thanks are owed to Jeanine, my family, and all my friends. Without them I could never have embarked on this interesting journey in the field of education.

This book is dedicated to my father.

CHAPTER ONE

THE COMPLEXITIES OF TEACHING

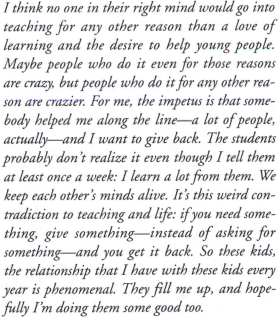

I think no one in their right mind would go into teaching for any other reason than a love of learning and the desire to help young people. Maybe people who do it even for those reasons are crazy, but people who do it for any other reason are crazier. For me, the impetus is that somebody helped me along the line—a lot of people, actually—and I want to give back. The students probably don't realize it even though I tell them at least once a week: I learn a lot from them. We keep each other's minds alive. It's this weird contradiction to teaching and life: if you need something, give something—instead of asking for something—and you get it back. So these kids, the relationship that I have with these kids every year is phenomenal. They fill me up, and hopefully I'm doing them some good too.

—Stanley, a sixth-year
California high-school English teacher[1]

BELIEVE THAT ALL TEACHERS want to become better at what they do. If you're reading this book, it must be because of your commitment to such an endeavor. You understand teaching to be a difficult but rewarding profession, and you're looking for ways to become a better teacher yourself. In this book, I hope to unravel the deep ways in which teachers grow and change and, in doing so, to uncover some of the hidden things that might be getting in the way of your own continued development and greater success. In the next hundred or so pages, I hope you'll find useful principles to apply to your own professional learning. If you engage the ideas of this book, reflect on them, and put them into practice, you will become a better educator.

You're likely to be somewhat knowledgeable about teaching and learning already—from your own time as a student, your professional preparation, prior teaching experiences you've had, or other work you've done with children. You already know many of the challenges to successful teaching. You've probably encountered several along the way, including some massive ones, such as societal reactions to your career choice, the maddening complexity of education, and the fact that schools are the places where society often plays out its never-ending cultural battles.

I hope that by reading this book you will learn how to get better at the hardest profession in the world. I believe that the more deeply you reflect on yourself as a teacher, the better you'll become at your work. Specifically, my focus in this book is on how multiple, often hidden, frequently personal influences on your own growth as a teacher are continually working to shape the educator you are—and are continually becoming. My hope is that if you can better understand the educator within yourself, then you can unlock your potential as a teacher and positively impact students in far greater ways than you ever imagined.

Building on my own research as well as on the research of others—and using as much wisdom of practice as I've accumulated during my work as a high-school English teacher, university teacher-educator, and education researcher—this book is meant to be its own teacher learning experience for you. The book introduces a model of teacher learning that illuminates how teachers—you, in this case—can systematically examine their own personal and professional teaching influences and work to adjust and assemble them in conjunction with education research into a coherent, successful whole. The result—that unique, successful whole—is what I call your teacher identity, and by better understanding it you will improve the kind of teacher you are in the classroom, the kind of learning you can offer your students, and the professional satisfaction you receive from your career.

COMPETING HISTORIES OF
TEACHING SHAPE YOUR WORK

Let's begin near the beginning. You've surely experienced dozens of reactions by others to your career choice—from the ambiguous "how nice" to the snarky "good luck with that"; from the slightly patronizing "that's so admirable" to the smug "why would you want to do *that*?" Most reassuring (and most truthful, in my opinion) is the insider's knowing response: "Welcome to the best and hardest profession in the world."

Hanging over all these replies, and a hundred well-traveled variations on them, is a series of competing histories of teaching in the United States. The various ways that teachers and teaching have been viewed over the past 150 years exert a powerful though often hidden influence on your own professional development. These sometimes parallel, sometimes reinforcing, often competing histories of teaching—separately and together, whether you know it or not—influence your own work. This is because at the same time that you are defining for yourself what it means to be a teacher, it is also continually being defined for you . . . by other educators, by your teaching environment, by students, by policymakers, and by the larger society. What are teachers "supposed to do"? What defines "good" or "bad" teachers? What does a "successful" classroom, school, or student look like? These are just a few of the broad questions on which past traditions of teaching still exert influence on your development as a teacher. They're worth examining.

One historical viewpoint of teaching is the old "if you can't do, then teach." This enduring view of teaching as *easy-entry, semiskilled work* defines teachers as those who couldn't succeed at anything else and so have stumbled into teaching. Of course it's offensive, and few actually utter the phrase in seriousness anymore, though its vestiges remain in characterizations of teachers as academically or intellectually weak, or as those who tried something lucrative or more challenging but couldn't succeed, or as people who crave their summers off. I won't deny that such teachers exist. But they aren't the norm, and there aren't enough of them to justify defining the profession in that way.

This distorted image remains partly because just about every adult has been a student and believes he or she knows what teaching is. From the vantage points and memories of members of the general public, teaching appears to be easy, protected, middle-status employment. Teaching is something that anyone can do. And the "clients" of teachers are children—among our most precious, but in practice least valued, resources. Additionally, people often think that all there is to teaching is the front-of-the-stage work (that is, performing, managing students, reading stories, making bulletin boards). All the behind-the-stage work (the years of preparation, the nightly reflection and weekend lesson planning, the time spent keeping up with current research) is invisible. Few people who are not teachers have ever considered just how much work takes place out of the audience's view.

Cross-Reference
For a related discussion on teacher responsibilities beyond the classroom, see Book 5, Chapter 3.

For them, teaching probably does look easy: only true teachers and those who are close to them know what's hidden away from the stage lights.

The second long-standing view of teaching is the notion that it is *predominantly women's work, akin to child-raising*. This idea has a particularly complicated history, being tangled up as it is in centuries-old notions of power, in population and demographic changes, and in sexism in the United States. The view holds at its core the myth that a woman's place is in the home and—the classroom being considered an extension of the home—that teaching is work for the nurturer, the matronly, the "softer side" of humanity. It holds that teaching is suitably nonintellectual, temporary, and low-paying work. Further, it perpetuates three circular falsehoods: that women are innately predisposed to teaching, that they are more interested in the charitable service of teaching as child-rearing than are men, and that women are content with mostly intrinsic rewards.

This women's-work viewpoint is also linked to an American history in which education has long sought to hire cheap labor for its classrooms: for much of the twentieth century, college-educated women had few professional options and so took what they could get, often at whatever price was offered. Education historian Marjorie Murphy (1990) has pointed out that in the early twentieth century, teaching represented a kind of aristocracy for women workers—a step up in status from the blue-collar worlds of their fathers, but one that lacked the ability to confer the power and sense of control held by males in positions of similar status, not to mention the relatively low pay. Prior to World War II, female urban teachers often lived as boarders in the homes of school board members, had to sign loyalty oaths, were required to be in before sundown, and were expected to leave the profession if they should marry. Pregnant teachers were considered bad role models, and lesbian women were not permitted to teach.

Consider the following commonly distributed contemporary hoax—a set of instructions for teachers, ostensibly from 1872; it isn't authentic (but rather an urban legend, and one found in classrooms just about everywhere!). I hesitate to include it, though its resonance marks some of the common conceptions of that time.

1872 INSTRUCTIONS TO THE TEACHERS

1. Teachers will fill lamps, clean chimneys, and trim wicks each day.
2. Each teacher will bring a scuttle of coal and a bucket of water for the day's use.
3. Make your pens carefully. You may whittle nibs for the individual tastes of children.
4. Men teachers may take one evening each week for courting purposes or two evenings a week if they go to church regularly.
5. After ten hours in the school the teacher should spend the remaining time reading the Bible and other good books.
6. Women teachers who marry or engage in other unseemly conduct will be dismissed.
7. Every teacher who smokes, uses liquor in any form, frequents pool or public halls, or gets

> shaved in a barber shop will give good reason to
> suspect his worth, intentions, integrity, and
> honesty.

Though it's doubtful that this patriarchal history led you
to choose teaching, I suspect that in various forms it has
shaped some of the contexts and roles of teaching in
which you find yourself today.

On a more positive side of the ledger in the history of
teaching, a third viewpoint sees teachers as content specialists with pedagogical expertise. This *professional, technical
view of teaching* began as early as Socrates. Its modern incar-
nation originated in the late nineteenth century with Euro-
pean theorists such as Friedrich Froebel and Jean Piaget
and moved into the early twentieth century with American
educationalists such as John Dewey, George Counts, and
Edward Thorndike before embedding itself into more recent school reform and teacher professionalization movements. This history frames teachers as experts in their fields
who possess deep content knowledge and relish success at
apprenticing young people into the fascinations and benefits of learning. It's a history that sees teachers as experts
who find joy in what they teach—literature, science, or
mathematics, for example, or the overall development of
children—and who strive to guide students into continually deepening views of themselves and the world around
them. It's also a history that gives us our current emphasis
on education testing.

This view of teaching is marked by an interest in the
pedagogical sciences and learning theory. Informed by
over a century of research on curriculum, instruction,
content knowledge, and assessment, it's a view of teachers
as experts who pay close attention to processes of learning
and teaching and find creative ways to help young people
construct their understandings of, and orientations to,
the world. This viewpoint treats teachers as well prepared,
knowledgeable, and committed—as professionals, in a
word. My guess is that this view of teaching—the chance

to know your subject well and guide your students successfully into its charms, challenges, and advantages—has
held sway for you.

Finally, there is a fourth broad history of teaching to
introduce: *noble work focused on democratic social change.*
This is another view of teaching that I suspect is salient
for you. It's connected to traditions of teaching as political, humanistic work. This viewpoint holds that teaching
is always a political act and wraps itself around progressive
social goals such as uplifting people from poverty, replac-
ing structural inequities with fairness, warmly embracing
diversity, and speaking truth to power. This view believes
that the democratic ideals of our country can, will, and
should be realized largely through education—in other
words, through you.

In 1967 Dr. Martin Luther King Jr. said, "Let us realize the arc of the moral universe is long, but it bends toward justice." Such a sentiment can remind teachers that
many of the social goals of education may take a long
time to become enacted, but that is no reason to concede
them. From freedom schools in the segregated South to
literacy movements for the working class, critical pedagogy, multiculturalism, and social-justice teaching, this
tradition of teaching as important, transformative work
for social change has ebbed and flowed over the decades,
and many teachers proudly embrace it.

Since the nineteenth century, these four histories of
teaching have become braided together in complex,
changing ways to form the shifting landscape of teaching
in the United States. Subtly but powerfully, these histories continue to inform many of the complexities of—
and disputes about—teaching that we experience today.
For example, the question of how schools should treat
immigrants and second-language learners can be interpreted in multiple ways depending on how one views the
larger purposes of education and the role of a teacher.
Additionally, contemporary disagreements around what
constitutes a "highly qualified teacher," whether to put

metal detectors in schools, or how to teach evolution are all concrete educational issues whose answers fundamentally depend on competing value systems and how participants define education. Historical views of teaching are still very active players in these educational debates.

As difficult as all this is to think about in the abstract, it's even more complex for a teacher to actually negotiate in daily practice. As a current or prospective teacher, you probably find yourself pulled in several directions by different, often contradictory conceptions of what a teacher is "supposed to" be and do. Moreover, any particular teaching context—the school culture, the characteristics of your community, the unique contours of your students and colleagues—carries its own influence. A teacher must negotiate among historical influences, contextual forces, the students in front of her, and her own goals and abilities in order to strike an effective teaching balance.

The primary task of this book is to draw attention to how the many contexts and histories of teaching interact with your own personal history to influence the kind of teacher you are becoming, or can become. It's my central premise that, as you examine for yourself the embedded processes of your own ongoing development, you will be able to more consciously and effectively shape who you are becoming as a professional educator. Just think about it: you have the unique power to shape your own professional growth, to become more satisfied in your professional life, to be more successful in the classroom, and to become the teacher you want to be—and that today's students intensely need you to be.

Focus point

TEACHING IS ALWAYS HARD WORK

No matter how you conceive of your chosen profession or how history has conceived it for you, teaching is difficult work. It's an enormously complex activity that is debated by almost everyone at every turn. Teaching requires use of the intellect, emotions, intuition, the senses, and judgment; knowledge of content, context, and kids; and kinesthetics, creativity, personality, and linguistic performance. Typically, several of these abilities combine; many times all twelve are called into simultaneous use. Teachers work with dozens of children at a time; the children typically vary in ability, maturity, background, and likeability—and many of them do not even want to be in school. Moreover, teaching occurs within multiple and often competing organizational, social, and political contexts exerting direct and indirect forces on what teachers think and do. Together, these constitute a tricky set of factors to manage, let alone control.

As I mentioned, just about everyone has been a student, and so the whole world believes it knows how teaching should be done. And we teachers hear this from everybody. Educators and noneducators alike are rarely shy about offering their opinions about teaching when we meet them in personal or professional settings. Additionally, school and district administrators, state and federal policymakers, and education stakeholders at many levels (including parents, politicians, professors, and pundits) all believe they know what's best for teachers and students. This combination makes for a constant push and pull, a tightening and loosening, a tangled ball of charged and active beliefs and policies that make up contemporary education in the United States and abroad. As David Cohen and Barbara Neufield (1981) wrote, "[Our] schools are a great theater in which we play out [the] conflicts in our culture." Furthermore, teachers are increasingly required to teach curricula created by others; they're sometimes pressured to teach in particular ways for reasons with which they may not agree; their professional status is often linked to student scores on standardized and sometimes misaligned tests. And the respect proffered to teachers seems perennially up for debate, as if teachers must continually defend themselves to everyone.

Our schools are a great theater in which we play out the conflicts in our culture.

Teachers, however, are not simply passive marionettes whose actions are governed by whoever holds the strings. Teachers have active agency, their own free will to enact their work as they see fit in order to make a difference in the lives of children. Sure, teachers are operated on by larger structures and forces, but they are also active agents able to make individual choices and teach in ways commensurate with their goals and philosophies of education. *Debates about how much power the structure (or institution) has over the individuals who exist within it—on the one side—and to what extent the individuals possess the power—on the other—have long been a popular research topic in education. In educational sociology, it's typically referred to as the "structure-agency debate."*

Focus point

Either way, teachers are the ones on whom most of the enormous burden of the complexities of education fall. Teachers are put in a contradictory position: They're supposed to follow orders and yet also be autonomous professionals. They're expected to serve the district bureaucracy but also students and families. Striking the balance isn't easy. As well, teachers are increasingly required to do their best with decreasing resources, eroding national support for public education, heightened surveillance, and an increasingly politicized education climate. As one teacher told me, "Teaching is a job with a lot of contradictions in it, and I think it requires a lot of perseverance and idealism. Without the idealism, you know, why would you be there?"

And yet, most teachers love what they do. We report that we "love working with kids," enjoy being able to "make a difference," appreciate being in an environment in which "everyone's constantly learning," "couldn't imagine doing anything else," and "have the dream job!" We talk about how wonderful it is to see the "lightbulb" of learning go on over a child's head, or the animated face of a student who just figured something out. We rhapsodize about the content we teach—the beauty of literature, the elegance of math, the transcendence of art, or the life-changing power of science, to name a few. We talk about watching students grow during their year with us. We praise our colleagues. We treasure cards, e-mails, and Facebook messages that we receive from former students and their parents who thank us for having done such a good job during an important time in their lives.

These gestures indeed keep us going, but we need to be honest with ourselves in that a thank-you note doesn't make us a better teacher, and neither does hard work alone. We must realize that, just as multiple pressures impact us daily as teachers, we are often unconsciously influenced by multiple past events in our lives that have shaped us as educators. In the following section I highlight some of those influences, hoping to expand your understanding of your own teacher development, and describe some tools you can use to shape yourself into the kind of teacher you want to become.

TEACHER EDUCATION AND PROFESSIONAL DEVELOPMENT

Teaching is complicated work, but so is *preparing and supporting teachers*. For decades, researchers have examined whether formal teacher education has an influence on the perspectives and practices of the teachers whom it prepares, and if so, how and to what extent. Consequently, there are thousands of studies on relationships between teacher education and teacher development. **Teacher education** is the formal process of teacher preparation, usually found in a university. **Teacher development** is the broader, more organic process of "becoming a teacher." It seems only logical that teachers who can recognize the influences exerted upon them by their teacher-preparation experiences will be able to better understand their own teacher identities.

Like teaching, teacher education can be characterized by a contested history and enduring complexities that shape the work. Historically, teacher-education programs

Key concept
teacher
education

Key concept
teacher
development

have come in all shapes and sizes, though they have mainly consisted of differing combinations of four primary approaches to the professional learning of teachers.[3] Sharon Feiman-Nemser (1990) named those four approaches the *academic orientation* (transmitting professional knowledge to the teacher), the *personal orientation* (focusing on the teacher's own development), the *critical orientation* (coupling social change with a radical critique of schooling), and the *technological orientation* (identifying what the science of teaching has uncovered).

These four models of teacher education have combined in various ways over the past hundred years. Most teacher-education programs participate to some degree in all four thematic strands, but each program tips its balance in favor of one or two at the expense of the others. For example, a program might focus on transmitting existing bodies of knowledge of teaching and learning to its students (the academic orientation) and supporting student teachers in their own individual growth (the personal orientation) without attending much to issues of race, class, power, or social change (the critical orientation). Or a program might focus almost exclusively on sociopolitical dimensions of schooling (the critical orientation) without much exposure to new research on methods of classroom teaching and learning (the technological and academic orientations). It's unlikely that you received a balanced approach in your teacher-education program. So an important aspect of understanding and shaping your teacher identity is to evaluate for yourself the predominant orientation of your program and then strive to fill in the resulting gaps that occurred in your preparation. In this way you can begin to direct your own professional development as a teacher.

Lately, teacher education as a whole has been under the political gun. Various pundits, politicians, and educators from both the political left and the right have called for complete overhauls, or the wholesale elimination of university teacher-education programs. Consider conservative columnist George Will (2006) claiming that "the surest, quickest way to add quality to primary and secondary education would be addition by subtraction: Close all the schools of education." A recent study released by the U.S. Department of Education that compared teachers prepared in university teaching programs with those who experienced alternate certification instead appears to have found virtually no differences in the achievement levels of their students (Constantine et al. 2009). Teacher-educators continually struggle with how best to help novice teachers become talented, knowledgeable, confident, well-prepared educators—and no single best answer has yet emerged.

DOES TEACHER EDUCATION INFLUENCE A TEACHER'S DEVELOPMENT?

Below I briefly review three well-known teacher-education studies that can help to illuminate some of the enduring personal tensions that often come into play during the beginning stages of teacher development. Though these research findings were published decades ago, they are still relevant and useful for new teachers. As you read about them, consider if—and how—they've played out for you.

Stages of Teaching Concern

In 1975, Frances Fuller and Oliver Bown wrote about the personal contradictions inherent in becoming a teacher. These two researchers found that becoming a teacher is "complex, stressful, intimate, and largely covert" and concluded that teacher-education programs aren't always adept at tending to the personally stressful aspects of a beginning teacher's development (1975, 2). For Fuller and Bown, teaching was largely about contradictions. For example, teachers are supposed to be themselves, but not too much—because they are, after all, agents of the state and public role models for kids. And teachers are supposed to change students' attitudes and habits, but since student characteristics often originate from home and society, teachers often find themselves competing against family beliefs and popular culture. For example, an equity-minded teacher might find herself competing against daily images and stereotypes from music, the Internet, and television that objectify and demean girls and model hypermasculinity for boys. Moreover, teacher education encourages teachers to be flexible and inventive, but schools often require conformity and standardization. These are just some of the inherent contradictions that make teaching difficult under even the best of circumstances.

Fuller and Bown presented four distinct stages of personal-professional concern for beginning teachers, arguing that one difficulty of becoming a teacher is that teacher education does not always address these concerns, or if it does, doesn't address them in the same sequence in which student teachers experience them. The four stages of teacher concern, which I summarize in Textbox 1.2, are meant to describe the clusters of personal-professional discomfort that novice teachers experience. It's difficult but necessary for new teachers to acknowledge and work through these phases during teacher education.

Fuller and Bown argued that teacher education leaves student teachers to confront these largely personal stages of their teaching development alone. This led the authors to conclude that formal teacher education is "a sort of fiddler crab dance, a ritual parallel to, but essentially irrelevant to, the real business of learning to teach" (1975, 5).

It's possible that your entry into teaching included (or will include) these frustrations. If so, being aware of them as they're occurring and making them objects of conversation with colleagues will help. Notice them, name them, and get others to talk about them with you.

An equity-minded teacher might find herself competing against daily images and stereotypes from music, the Internet, and television that objectify and demean girls and model hypermasculinity for boys.

TEXTBOX 1.2

First stage: Pre-teaching concerns. Beginning teachers (often in their early twenties and slightly rebellious in temperament) identify more with students than with other teachers and face a troubling authority bind when they enter the classroom: they view their entry into teaching as "going over to the enemy." They struggle to accept their role as the authority because they would rather be the students' friend.

Second stage: Survival concerns. Novice teachers are mostly concerned with just getting through the day. This kind of survival mode pushes the deeper aspects of teaching and learning into the background as novices focus on being liked, managing the class, and avoiding mistakes. Being a deeply reflective teacher is postponed until later when day-to-day routines become more established.

Third stage: Teaching-situation concerns. Novice teachers feel overwhelmed by all the noninstructional work of teaching, such as being sure to follow school policies, doing paperwork, and finding sufficient materials. The focus on the logistical dimensions of teaching (such as working the copy machine) precludes deep attention to teaching and learning.

Fourth stage: Student concerns. Novice teachers, now finally becoming able to attend to the students in front of them, begin to worry that they cannot know and focus on all the needs of their many students. They may feel that their wonderful students deserve a more accomplished teacher, or that they have too many students to teach well. They feel guilty because they believe their students deserve better.

If you're aware that they're common (it's not just you!) and that they will pass (I promise!), it's easier to manage them. To consider how their subtle contours are being shaped by—and are shaping—who you are as an educator is to begin to gain some control over them.

The Concept of "Washout"

Kenneth Zeichner and Robert Tabachnick (1981) were interested in examining the claim that beginning teachers may not be much changed by their teacher-education experience. These two researchers investigated a puzzling phenomenon: beginning teachers seem to exhibit few, if any, of the progressivist, liberal approaches their university programs espouse. Why is that? How can teacher educators advocate progressive notions of teaching only to find their graduates teaching in traditional, conservative ways—seemingly unchanged by the formal preparation experience?

One explanation offered was that teacher-education programs do, in fact, nudge student teachers toward liberal educational beliefs and progressive pedagogies. Yet the K–12 schools in which graduates subsequently find themselves carry such strong traditional socializing forces that the effects of university teacher-education programs are essentially "washed out" by the socialization of the school. Teachers are mostly powerless against the histories and structures of education and, soon enough, will teach the way their workplaces are organized. Since most educational workplaces are organized around traditional learning and teaching methods, the teachers who enter the schools, no matter how they were trained, quickly slide into acceptance of the dominant practices of the school, thus becoming the "traditional" kinds of teachers they once opposed.

A second explanation that Zeichner and Tabachnick put forward was that washout occurs because teachers are shaped mostly by their own biographies as students, not by their teacher-education programs. Many beginning teachers were exposed to traditional instructional methods for most of their student lives, so the traditional view becomes their default philosophy of teaching. Against that prevailing force, teacher-education programs are relatively powerless. Novice teachers may adopt the language or surface

practices of progressive teaching in their programs—
perhaps to gain instructor approval, or because they're
temporarily seduced by the intellectual charms of education theory—but this rhetoric is superficial and fades once
they begin teaching, and they return to the more traditional, deeply embedded pedagogies with which they grew
up. As Francis O'Connoll Rust wrote, teacher education is
"but a patina of beliefs layered over a lifetime of learning"
(Rust 1994). This argument holds that teachers teach how
they were taught, and attempts to dislodge these familiar
practices will often fail.

The third explanation Zeichner and Tabachnick offered was that, in fact, there is indeed an alignment between the student teachers and their university programs,
but it's conservative on both sides. In other words, university teacher-education programs may appear on the
surface to be liberal or progressive, but below that they are
actually quite traditional in their education practices. The
teacher-educators are "talking the talk" without "walking
the walk." Though they may employ the language and
theoretical trappings of progressive education (for example, students should construct their own knowledge,
learning by rote doesn't work, cultural diversity is an as-
set), their own practices actually rely on traditional notions of learning and teaching (for example, knowledge is
external to the learner, experts deliver preselected information to students, lecturing is best). And they may tout
social-justice principles around race, culture, and power
in education, but they do not live up to these ideals.

Zeichner and Tabachnick didn't offer an opinion on
which explanation was the most accurate but wrote that
each view had "some credibility" (10). Also, their review
of the literature is now almost thirty years old and definitions of terms such as *liberal, conservative,* and *traditional* have changed since then. But the broader
questions they raised are still relevant and have been continually updated and refined by researchers ever since.

Given these enduring complexities, it's important for
you to stop and spend some time reflecting on whether

any of these three models of teacher-education washout are true for you. Consider what kind of teacher experience you had (or are currently having). How was it related to what you thought teaching was when you first entered the teacher-education program? Furthermore, as you find yourself working as a teacher in a school, it's important to consciously choose—to the degree that you can—the ways you will allow the school culture to influence your teacher identity and, conversely, to identify those aspects of the school's influence that you want to actively resist. You can in fact determine the extent to which you will actively seek to shape the contexts in which you teach instead of letting those contexts shape you—but more on this point later in the book.

PITFALLS OF PERSONAL EXPERIENCE

Sharon Feiman-Nemser and Margret Buchmann (1985) defined three "pitfalls of experience in teacher preparation" to describe ways in which student teachers err by relying on prior experience during their teacher education. The authors pointed out that they were in a sense debunking the axiom that "experience is the best teacher." Instead, Feiman-Nemser and Buchmann argued, learning from personal experience can be problematic because it escapes critical interrogation, because it sometimes houses misconceptions passed down throughout history, and because it hasn't been formally or systematically tested.

One of the three pitfalls is the *familiarity pitfall*—the idea that we automatically give extra credence to what we're familiar with, such as the supposed truism that an orderly class is a successful class or the one holding that any student answer is either right or wrong and it's the teacher's job to decide which. We are quick to accept something as true if it correlates with what we already know. For example, what seems like a noisy and chaotic classroom is something our automatic self might find problematic and determine to avoid—because that's been our experience. But in fact some education research suggests that noisy "chaos" may actually be a sign of authentic learning and naturally engaged students. Since we've been students in dozens of classrooms with dozens of different teachers, we might think that we've seen it all before and know what it all means. As soon as we draw that conclusion, we begin activating our own memories as learning source rather than fully engaging the possibility of new and different kinds of learning. As a result, we might fall into the trap of unthinkingly teaching as we were taught, or overvaluing the so-called common sense of things in the classroom.

The second pitfall is the *two-worlds pitfall*. This describes the habit of constructing a mental separation between the university world and the world of the K–12 classroom. It's akin to the popular but erroneous theory-practice divide: the myth that studying a thing is completely disconnected from doing the thing. Student teachers believe that what happens in university teacher-preparation programs is mostly abstract or esoteric learning and that the real learning, the true crucible of teacher development, is the time spent teaching in the classroom. Pitting the two "worlds" against each other, these authors argued, creates an ethos in which university education courses and research become downgraded against the value of hands-on experience. It's one reason we too often hear experienced teachers saying that a teacher-education program doesn't teach you much; what those teachers are often trying to say is that they believe education theory doesn't actually help someone teach. Generally, the two-worlds pitfall neglects the integrated nature of both "learning" and "doing": in truth, learning *is* doing and doing *is* learning. This theory-practice divide is a topic I will take up in more detail in Chapter 2.

The third pitfall that Feiman-Nemser and Buchmann identified is one they call the *cross-purposes pitfall*. This is the mistaken belief that *learning to teach* is a vastly different process from *teaching*. It asserts that, for many student teachers, "learning to teach" is about trying new approaches, making mistakes along the way, thinking experimentally—while "teaching" is mostly about getting through the day with as few mistakes as possible and "acting like" a successful teacher. If classrooms aren't typically considered places to *learn to teach* (but instead as places *where teaching occurs*), the authors argued, then classrooms become viewed by student teachers as primarily places in which to prove oneself. If adopted, this belief can lead student teachers to underprivilege their own authentic development and to overprivilege surviving, impressing observers, or enacting teaching as an artificial performance on the public stage of a classroom. By not taking risks and trying out new pedagogies, they will lose the opportunity to grow as teachers.

Feiman-Nemser and Buchmann's three pitfalls are like blindspots to an automobile driver: places where one's vision is blocked. Beginning teachers often enter their teacher-education experience already armed with conceptions—myths even—that hinder their ability to critically view and confront their prior experience while learning new ways to think about teaching. We educators should be grateful for, but wary of, our prior experience. If it is true, as pianist Bill Evans has said, that "all experience enters into you" (Pettinger 1998), then each of us is, in part, a product of our experiences. But as teachers we should not be imprisoned by them. We must act as conscious gatekeepers, determining *which* of our experiences will carry influence for us and *how* we let them do their work on us.

WHAT ABOUT PROFESSIONAL DEVELOPMENT?

Just as teacher education is designed to alter and deepen the views and practices of entering teachers, so too is *professional development* intended to support teacher growth. But rather than focusing on pre-service student teachers, professional development targets in-service teachers who

Focus point

are already working in schools. And, just as teacher education doesn't always accomplish its intended effects, neither does professional development. Its influence, too, is contingent upon how the individual teacher chooses to make use of it. **Professional development** describes the various programs, workshops, and networks that cater to practicing teachers (and their schools) to help them improve their teaching, learn new curricula, and continually develop as educators.

The better you can understand and control your own teacher learning—whether it derives from your personal history, your teacher-education experience, your teaching itself, or professional development—the more use you can make of the opportunities offered you. Teachers who do not actively use the professional development offered them will not be much helped by it. Tied to the premise of this book is the principle that the best way to make use of professional development is to engage in it in tandem with focused, critical reflection on your teacher identity: a task this book will attempt to teach you how to carry out.

Over the past decade or so, research has found that older models of professional development—one- or two-day workshops in which hired presenters talk through new materials or new ways of teaching to faculty members sitting in the school auditorium—don't work very well. Two important changes in professional development have recently occurred: a shift toward ongoing, off-site, teacher-chosen professional development networks, and a view of teacher careers as holistic. Let's take a look at that second change first.

In the past, people, organizations, and research studies focused on any one of those phases, with only passing attention to its relationship with the others. For example, professional development typically did not take into account why a teacher had entered the profession or the differing ways that particular participating teachers had been trained. Instead, each teacher at any point in his or her career was treated more or less like a blank slate onto which new learning could easily be written.

TEXTBOX 1.3

We once treated careers in teaching as a series of mostly discrete, sequenced phases and in doing so suggested that each stage of a teacher's career was different from the other stages. Those phases included recruitment (bringing prospective teachers into the profession), pre-service teacher education (the training of novices), an early period (called "induction"), the professional development phase (the main part of one's career), and one's longevity in the profession.

Phases of a Teaching Career

- Teacher recruitment (attracting people into the profession)
- Pre-service teacher education (preparing novice teachers)
- Induction (supporting beginning teachers through their first year or two)
- In-service professional development (professional improvement for working teachers)
- Teacher retention (keeping good teachers in the profession)

It has become increasingly evident, however, that each phase influences and impacts the others. For example, teachers' reasons for entering the profession might shape how they learn from their pre-service programs, which in turn may shape how they will evaluate the schools where they work and how they feel about remaining in or leaving the profession of teaching over the long haul. Or perhaps the specific contours of an individual teacher's preparation program might affect what kind of professional development he or she will find helpful later on. In addition, researchers have noticed that in this current day and age, many teachers come into the profession after already having had one career, might leave teaching for a time (to have children, for example) and then return, or might continually shift around to work in several education jobs over the course of their career (Moore Johnson et al. 2004; Quartz et al. 2010 in this series).

Given this acknowledgment of the interconnectedness of the phases and the shifting nature of teaching careers, many researchers and professional development specialists have begun viewing teacher development as more of a continuum. The once-separate domains of recruitment, pre-service preparation, induction, in-service professional development, and teacher retention are now being put into active conversation with each other. This idea has inspired new approaches to professional development. It also helps to inform this book's view that improving one's quality as a teacher requires looking deeply at how all the constituent parts of one's professional identity combine to contribute to the practice of teaching. The useful effects of professional development on you as a teacher will only be as good as your ability to make use of—to engage with and grow from—the experiences you are offered and the experiences you seek out. This means that, like teacher education and learning from your own teaching practice, professional development is mediated by your own unique teacher identity.

One recent trend in professional development is *teacher-chosen, ongoing, professional networks* that support teachers throughout their career. These networks include critical inquiry groups, critical friends, university-supported networks for alumni teachers, and online teacher communities. The principle behind this approach is that these groups are their own "communities of practice" where professionals form *lasting, productive relationships* as they talk together about their daily work and collaborate on ways to frame, address, and concretely solve their teaching dilemmas—sometimes even collaborating on their teaching practice (see, for example, Freedman et al. 1999; Lieberman and Wood 2006). A second trend is *project-based professional development*—tying these teaching conversations and new learning opportunities to *actual, shared educational projects*. Some examples of project-based professional development are action research (teachers researching their own practice), curriculum development, online video sharing, and instigation of schoolwide initiatives such as a parent project or a community garden (see Anderson and Olsen 2006).

To push the notion of a continuum of teacher development even further, I propose a more circular, continuous notion of teacher development and careers. Rather than the image of a teacher's career as a horizontal line—with each phase chronologically sequenced in a forward-moving fashion—I suggest an intricately interconnected circle: an image of the teaching career that is more like a spring washer that you might purchase in a hardware store (see Figure 1.1).[4]

A teacher's career certainly proceeds chronologically; that is, the teacher lived part of his or her life before entering teaching ("one's biography" above), started formal teacher learning at the beginning of the teaching career ("teacher ed experience"), and will work as a teacher one year at a time ("being a teacher")—growing incrementally along the way. This connectedness, what I previously described as a continuum, is represented in Figure 1.1 by the outside arrows, which suggest chronological movement. The circle does not close, however, because a teacher's career actually ends at some point in time. The continuous nature of most of the circle emphasizes that

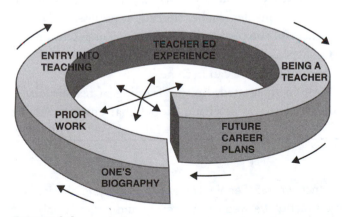

FIGURE 1.1

the phases of a teacher's work are not distinct segments but rather points along a seamless, *forward-moving* career.

But in terms of a teacher's knowledge and professional identity—those deeper ways in which a teacher is at any given moment interpreting, enacting, and reflecting on his or her work—*all the parts are always in use.* This interconnectivity of the parts is represented by the arrows inside the figure. As we teach and think about our teaching, we're automatically drawing on past goals, memories, and reasons for entry; our biographies, present perspectives, and work contexts; and predictions for our professional future.

This more circular notion of professional development highlights the interconnectedness of phases of a teaching career—a view where each phase is continually influencing and being influenced by the others. All these parts of a teacher's identity are continually in play—sometimes receding into the background and other times becoming dominant, but always interacting to influence how, in the flow of activity, a teacher conceives of and enacts his or her teaching. John Muir (1911) famously wrote that, "when we try to pick out anything by itself, we find it hitched to everything else in the Universe" (Muir 1911, 110). That is certainly true of a teacher's identity: who we are as teachers is hitched to who we are as humans, which itself is hitched to our own lived experiences. As a result, we need to consider teacher education, professional development, and the personal-professional changes and needs of teachers as integrated and interconnected parts of who we are and what we can become.

Such an integrated, holistic framing of teacher development aligns well with a model that emphasizes the

Cross-Reference For a discussion on teacher development and personal experience, see Book 5, Chapter 1.

TEXTBOX 1.4

Albert Einstein once wrote: "People like us, who believe in physics, know that the distinction between past, present, and future is only a stubbornly persistent illusion."

whole teacher as a deep, complicated human being of multiple sources and influences that are continually being assembled and reassembled in ways that shape a teacher's view of his or her work. This model highlights the fact that teachers' professional development requires that they acknowledge and actively use their unique, holistic, professional selves. This book shows you how you can do just that.

CONCLUSION

Now that you have some understanding of the foundations of what helps to make us who we are as teachers, I want to focus on what matters most: how you can become the best teacher you can be. The way to do this is for you to raise your awareness and understanding about the deeply embedded, long-held beliefs you have about teaching—coming largely from your personal history—that you are uniquely assembling into a workable whole. This "whole" is what we might call a teacher's professional self. For reasons I'll explain in the next chapter, I prefer the term *teacher identity*.[5]

DISCUSSION QUESTIONS

1. Why did you enter the teaching profession? Are these reasons still important to you now? How might these reasons for entry have shaped the ways you currently view teaching?

2. How would you characterize your own teacher-education program? What did it do well? What aspects of teaching and learning might it have left out? How will you fill in those gaps in your professional preparation?

3. What kinds of professional development have you experienced? What did they teach you? From what kinds of professional development do you find that you learn the most?

4. How would you describe yourself as a teacher? What are the primary characteristics of your current teacher identity?

FURTHER READING

Clifford, G., and J. Guthrie. 1988. *Ed School.* Chicago: University of Chicago Press.

Cochran-Smith, M., and K. Zeichner, eds. 2005. *Studying Teacher Education: The Report of the AERA Panel on Research and Teacher Education.* Mahwah, NJ: Lawrence Erlbaum Associates.

Cuban, L. 1993. *How Teachers Taught: Constancy and Change in American Classrooms.* New York: Teachers College Press.

Lieberman, A., and L. Miller. 2008. *Teachers in Professional Communities: Improving Teaching and Learning.* New York: Teachers College Press.

NOTES

1. A note about teachers' names in this book: Sometimes the names of the teachers I quote are pseudonyms to ensure confidentiality; other times the names are teachers' actual names. It depends on the research circumstances in which the interviews were conducted.

2. Thanks to Dan Perlstein for sharing this information with me.

3. There are, of course, many different models and structures of teacher preparation (for example, undergraduate teaching pathways, graduate or "5th-year" credentialing programs, and various field-based internships or alternative entries into teaching such as Teach for America or the NYC Teaching Fellows program). Furthermore, there are myriad nuances, contradictions, and loose ends associated with teacher education. It's neither as monolithic nor as coherent as my summary suggests. For more, see Clifford and Guthrie 1988; Cochran-Smith and Zeichner 2005.

4. Thanks to Lou Waddell for creating all graphics in this book.

5. Parts of some of these chapters (especially Chapter 3) come from a previously published work of mine, *Teaching What They Learn, Learning What They Live: How Teachers' Personal Histories Shape Their Professional Development* (Boulder: Paradigm Publishers, 2008). Permission to reprint has generously been given.

CHAPTER TWO

KNOWLEDGE, LEARNING, AND IDENTITY FOR TEACHERS

A huge thing about how I'm a better teacher now, compared to when I began, is that I know a lot more now, and the things that I know I use differently in the classroom. So it's like I know more, I know differently, and I'm more reflective about how I know what I know. It makes every-thing better. I wish I was like this before.

—Nancy, a ninth-year California high school social studies teacher

IN CHAPTER 1, I made the case for why it's impera-tive that teachers enter into a reflective process about their own teacher identities. In this chapter I look at how beginning teachers construct their professional knowledge—how they learn to become teachers. I've chosen to focus on *knowledge* because it's a central part of any teacher's overall development (though, as we shall see, it's not the only important part). As you think about how your own teacher knowledge continually develops, you'll be better able to critically examine the many disparate influences on your teacher identity and the ways in which they interrelate. This should position you to consciously shape your development as an educator. Put more simply: only by becoming aware of your learning processes will you gain some control over them.

What we know as teachers, how we came to know it, and how our knowledge guides our practice are topics that sit at the center of our educational work. That makes them important questions to examine, because reflection on these questions can act as a lever for change. As we become aware of *how* we are acquiring our teaching knowledge, we can better evaluate, adjust, and reassemble our knowledge in ways that improve our teaching. In fact, *this is how I define "teacher learning": not only as teachers gaining new knowledge but as teachers becoming wiser about their past and current knowledge and how they're using it.* In this chapter I explain how teachers develop their professional understandings. More specifically, I review some of the central ways in which researchers and theorists have viewed knowledge. I also examine a popular debate about teacher learning and put forward my model of teacher identity as an alternative to traditional models of teacher learning.

Focus point

LEARNING TO TEACH: A RESEARCH HISTORY

It's important to begin with some key understandings of how people learn to teach. The modern era of research on teacher learning began about thirty-five years ago with a new focus on teacher cognition. As a backlash against what they believed had been an overly behavioristic approach to the study of teaching, several education theorists in the 1970s began conducting research on *teacher thinking* (Clark and Yinger 1979; Good et al. 1975; Shavelson and Stern 1981). These researchers began asking questions such as "How does a teacher's thinking relate to student achievement?" "Do novice teachers and expert teachers think about teaching differently?" and "What does an effective teacher know?" *Teacher knowledge* researchers picked this up in the 1980s and 1990s and started asking, "What is a teacher's knowledge base?" "Where does it come from?" and "What does a teacher need to know in order to be successful?" (see, for example, Shulman 1986). (In truth, these are important questions that all good educators should keep asking themselves every teaching day.)

Simultaneously, the concept of *action research* (sometimes called teacher research) has long encouraged teachers to become researchers of their classrooms. Action research not only offers evidence-based ways for teachers to improve their own practice but also, if done well, enriches larger bodies of education knowledge and theory (Cochran-Smith and Lytle 1993). In addition, action research has a valuable political function because it challenges existing views about where, and by whom, teaching knowledge is created, often arguing that teacher knowledge derives from teachers in classrooms as much as from professors in universities. In reality, educational researchers conducting rigorous studies *and* practitioners carefully examining and reporting on their own practice have much to offer the teaching profession.

TEXTBOX 2.1

One long-standing debate in educational research is over the relative value of the "outsider looking in" concept as a useful approach to inquiry versus the "practitioner looking at things for herself." This debate is linked to philosophical claims of objectivity and positivism, on the one side, and postmodernism and political critiques of traditional research, on the other. My belief is that in the aggregate all views on teaching and all vantage points have something to contribute to the knowledge base on teaching and teacher development. What's important is to examine the methodological strengths and weaknesses of the various approaches at the same time their results are being considered for use.

And, finally, contributions from *critical theory* have introduced consideration of how language, power, and sociocultural contexts influence the ways in which humans reflect on and enact their knowledge, thinking, and learning (Bourdieu 1991; Foucault 1970, 1977; Popkewitz and Brennan 1998). This loosely connected cluster of theories has long highlighted active roles that social relations, politics, history, and resulting balances of power play in any aspect of social life, including education. Applied to a teacher's knowledge, this critical-theory perspective becomes a useful framework for educators who focus on power relations to explain schooling, learning, and what it means to be a teacher. This set of views also beckons all of us to more thoroughly examine our own relationships to race, culture, gender, sexual orientation, and power and how they profoundly shape our teaching—a topic that is considered more fully in Chapter 6 of this book.

WHAT IS EDUCATION KNOWLEDGE?

Within the research on teaching, a long-standing question exists about where teaching knowledge resides. Is it located in the minds of teachers who are constantly generating, testing, and relying on their own theories about their work? Or is it located in books and articles from professors and researchers who apply systematic research methods to educational phenomena and report what they find? If professional knowledge is located mostly inside teachers, then preparing and supporting teachers is a question of encouraging them to develop, tap into, and effectively harness what they already know and experience. If, however, such knowledge is located mostly in research findings and published theories, then teacher development is about providing teachers with opportunities to access and internalize the research so they can effectively apply this new knowledge to their classroom situations. Let's take a closer look at this issue as you begin to ponder your own position on this debate.

"Theory" versus "theory"

For me, a useful way to think about this tension is to consider that *practice always follows from some kind of theory*. Whether or not we acknowledge it, people's choices and behaviors are mostly governed by their various embedded views of the world. Adult learning, then, becomes the process of examining what understandings of the world you are actually relying on and making conscious decisions about whether to retain, jettison, or adjust your deeper views. Specialized knowledge involves the same process, although framed more narrowly and technically. And instincts and biological urges are something else altogether (Wilson 2004).

Before we go into the further details of teacher knowledge, it seems useful to consider what we mean when we talk about "theory" in relation to education. I have often seen beginning teachers recoil when the word "theory" is used in their presence. As students in a teacher-preparation program, they fear that any reference to theory means they're going to be inundated by dense, boring reading material that makes education more complicated than it needs to be and may not even contain any useful implications for practice. "What does this have to do with actually teaching?" they inevitably ask. "How will I use this in my classroom tomorrow?" "Why does the author write in such an obfuscating way?" They may report, "My cooperating teacher tells me you don't learn anything in courses like this one." As working teachers or student teachers, they flinch and gird themselves for what they believe will be an overly abstract or irrelevant conversation.

When this occurs in my courses, I try to demystify the very concept of theory. I suggest that "theory" simply points to the fact that people's actions in the world are largely informed by their underlying understandings of the world (even if the process of relying on those understandings is largely automatic). When I'm cooking in the kitchen, for example, I'm operating on understandings of what heat does to food, how much force is needed on the knife, whether this amount of broth will fit into that bowl, and how long it will take to roast those vegetables in that oven at this temperature. Whether or not I know the science of cooking, I know enough to make certain predictions and adjust my practice accordingly. I'm operating on theory as I make choices and take action. My personal ideas about how to cook successfully are both related to and different from the body of knowledge derived from researchers who study the effects of heat on molecules, the physics of objects, or how sugars morph into energy during digestion.

One way of approaching the debate about where teacher knowledge comes from, then, might be to call that first category of knowledge "theory" with a small "t," and the second category "Theory" with a big "T" (a distinction that I will use only in this section). Lowercase "theory," then, would be the personal, experience-based, somewhat idiosyncratic ideas about teaching, learning, and schooling that an individual teacher might rely on to understand and act in the world as an educator. It might be fueled as much by intuitions, memories, and opinions—or "folk theories" as Feiman-Nemser and Buchmann (1985) call it—as by professional perspectives, educational research, and systematic critical reflection. I have found that lowercase "theory" is the guiding system for many classroom teachers. This worries me. Lowercase theory is almost automatic, rarely noticed as anything other than a kind of "common sense" or "wisdom of practice," and is hard to dislodge, because it's rarely made visible for examination.

It's also sometimes criticized for being dominated by society's prevailing norms, ideological prejudices, or naïve opinions. We all would like to think that if a teacher is a good person, works hard, and truly loves kids, then everyone in the class will learn well. The real world of education, however, proves more complex than simple maxims might allow.

Uppercase "Theory," in contrast, consists of those claims about the world that are generated and disseminated (that is, systematically hypothesized, tested, adjusted, and published) by professional researchers following standardized methods of inquiry. An example of this kind of social science could be Luis Moll and his colleagues' notion of "funds of knowledge." "Funds of knowledge" refers to a set of research findings about working-class Latino families in the United States who, like most non-Latino families, engage in multiple kinds of higher-order cognitive tasks all day long as they navigate their lives. Managing home finances, coordinating multiple schedules, and navigating multiple language and translation duties are all extremely complicated tasks requiring complex mental and emotional work. Yet, unlike the stores of knowledge of most middle-class Anglo families, many of these Latino "funds of knowledge" are rarely called upon for daily use by the schools their children attend (Gonzalez et al. 2005). "Funds of knowledge," then, is a Theory related to how teachers can find ways to identify and include in the classroom the historically undervalued cognitive capacities that Latino children engage in daily.

Uppercase Theory is sometimes criticized for being too abstract, rarefied, or full of soaring generalities. As a result, some teachers who read about this concept of "funds of knowledge" might not be able to make a meaningful connection to their daily work in the classroom. It is also often suggested that, just because it's found and reported by so-called professional researchers doesn't make Theory necessarily accurate. Critics argue that Theory may well be slanted toward the dominant ideologies and cultural meaning systems held by the researchers themselves or by their funding agencies. Some of these criticisms might hold partial truth, but we should be careful not to simplify the issue to an all-or-nothing mindset in regard to lowercase and uppercase theory.

In my opinion, both a person's personal educational theories and the Theory generated by educational researchers are important for teachers. Informed professionals move along in the world by successfully integrating both into the practice of teaching. This means that acknowledging and directing the way your own theories become integrated with larger Theories of education as you develop as a teacher should reap great benefits for you, both professionally and personally.

COGNITIVE AND SITUATED THEORIES OF LEARNING

One powerful question within the debate about how teachers *learn to teach* is the question of whether knowledge is constructed in context or acquired in the abstract. In other words: Is "knowledge" a *thing*—a body of understandings—that is formed and then passed down from experts to novices? Or is it an *activity*—a set of ongoing practices and accompanying conceptions—in which participating people learn to view the world in new ways? Put another way, we need to ask ourselves whether knowledge is a product or a process.

This is not just a hollow, academic debate. It has real consequences for how educators frame their own learning. What a teacher educator, or teacher, or school administrator believes about how teachers learn will shape how resources are used, how practices are structured, how teacher growth is measured, and what behaviors are rewarded. It's my contention that all of us have a responsibility to do some hard thinking about our own positions on what learning is and then continuously examine and evaluate those positions.

The scholarly debate about whether learning is cognitive or situated—to use the research terminology—is profound and long-standing. At its center lies disagreement about whether the primary entity involved in learning is the *isolated individual* or the *group in a context. This debate between situated and cognitive theories of*

Focus point

learning is sometimes termed as a debate between "individual" and "social" perspectives, or between "cognitive constructivism" and "sociocultural constructivism." In addition, the situated perspective is often discussed within the context of "sociocultural learning theory." (For more on this topic, see Anderson et al. 2000; Fosnot 2005; Lave and Wenger 1991; Oakes and Lipton 2006.) The cognitive tradition locates learning inside *internal cognitive processes*—in other words, information-processing mechanisms inside an individual's mind that are believed to connect external stimuli with individual responses. This cognitive perspective does not ignore the role of context (or its synonym, "environment") but views context—or the "task and relevant features of the setting" (Cobb and Bowers 1999)—as an *influence on* learning, rather than as part of the learning itself. This tradition could be aligned with metaphors of learning such as the single "lightbulb" going off above a learner's head, or the notion of "finally getting it"—as if the "it" is out there in the world waiting for a learner to finally internalize it.

Some scholars, however, critique this view of learning as overly narrow and limited by its lack of attention to the roles of context, culture, and social relationships. Several of these researchers instead view learning as occurring firmly inside *the interaction between individual(s) and environment* (Anderson et al. 2000; Lave 1988; Lave and Wenger 1991). These social theorists put forward a situated perspective on learning that takes as a primary unit of analysis an "interactive system composed of groups of individuals together with the material and representational resources they use" (Cobb and Bowers 1999). Here, learning is perceived entirely as a *social activity*, within an actual context, in which participants begin to think in new ways, undergo identity shifts, adopt new ways of using language, and produce new memories. "Learning," then, becomes the interconnected, grounded, fundamentally social ways in which people construct meaning out of experience.

One example might be two teachers trading ideas back and forth with such enthusiasm and mutual respect that, by the end of their brainstorming session, they don't know which ideas were whose—but they have both acquired new understandings and leave the interaction with new knowledge.

Social theorists Jean Lave and Etienne Wenger wrote that such a view of learning "impl[ies] emphasis on comprehensive understanding involving the whole person rather than 'receiving' a body of factual knowledge about the world; on activity in and with the world; and on the view that agent, activity, and the world mutually constitute each other" (Lave and Wenger 1991, 33).

Though both sides (except for extremists at each end) agree that learning is a process of constructing a new thing out of available materials, the cognitive perspective treats knowledge more as a thing, while the situated perspective treats it as a process. The cognitive perspective presumes that knowledge can be constructed within one context yet easily transferred to and employed in another context. The situated perspective assumes that, because knowledge and context are inextricably related, knowledge does not transfer but rather is reconstructed anew each time. You might be asking yourself, why is this topic important to me? The answer is that if teachers don't fully understand the process of learning, it will be extremely difficult for them to maximize student efforts to construct learning of their own.

As a teacher, your understanding of learning theory guides your teaching practice. Consider whether you tend to emphasize knowledge as an entity that gets passed along from teacher to student (or from textbook to reader), or view knowledge as a process by which people in social settings formulate their own unique understandings of the world. Consider whether you privilege students working alone, quietly attempting to master the material, or prefer to have students working together in groups trying to solve learning dilemmas.

The Learning Debate Applied to Teacher Development

Traditionally, the two competing perspectives about learning—and the tension between them—have shaped approaches to teacher education and professional development. Those who presume that learning is primarily cognitive could accept, for example, a definition of teacher knowledge as proved theory taught to beginning teachers and applied appropriately by those teachers to classroom situations. Such a view supports the loosely assembled bundle of conceptions, curricula, and pedagogies common within most twentieth-century teacher-education programs in the United States: pre-service teachers learned theories and teaching approaches in university classrooms for a semester, and then they practiced and internalized them in some kind of supervised teaching practicum. This has been the dominant model of teacher education for a long time. Student teachers are expected to absorb bodies of educational knowledge and then find ways to apply that knowledge as a successful set of teaching practices that will work in most any classroom. This approach, though, rests on two shaky premises: that learning takes place primarily in the mind of the individual learner, and that knowledge transfers relatively intact.

If, instead, we accept that the process of teacher learning is often situated, then it means we presume that teachers construct their own knowledge out of their various activities and contexts. This means that a teacher's knowledge and a teacher's knowledge process are inextricably linked to his or her lived experiences. If we grant this, it follows that we must view each teacher as a unique and three-dimensional learner—someone who combines life, learning, and practice to create personalized understandings of, and relationships to, the world and him- or herself. Who one is as a person affects who one is as both a learner and a teacher. Life and learning intertwine.

We must view each teacher as a unique and three-dimensional learner—someone who combines life, learning, and practice to create personalized understandings of, and relationships to, the world and him- or herself.

Such a view is often invoked to characterize apprenticeship models of teacher education that stress problem-posing curricula, communities of practice, and an emphasis on pre-service teachers interrogating their personal influences (Dewey 1904, 1933; Darling-Hammond et al. 1995; Oakes and Lipton 2006). This model includes teacher-educators who emphasize critical reflection for teachers—finding ways to encourage student teachers to examine their own selves and locations in society—or programs that rely on actual teaching case studies or videos to pose and instigate discussion on teaching dilemmas that beginners will soon face. These approaches rest on the premises that (1) learning takes place within the whole person always acting inside a unique setting, and (2) knowledge is inextricably linked to context. They are at times criticized for allowing students' own naïve views to dominate learning, or for encouraging excessive "navel gazing." And they are sometimes criticized for relying on a determinism that presumes that people are prisoners of their own experience.

So, that's the dichotomous version of this debate: learning occurs mostly in one's mind, or learning is mostly constructed out of one's participation in some environment. And, oddly, participants of the scholarly debate rarely posit legitimate places in between these two extremes. In order to treat learning in ways both deep and broad, I choose to accept that it's really a combination of both views of learning. Separately, each perspective illuminates a different, fundamental aspect of learning and, together, both perspectives complement each other to illuminate how teachers develop (and how learners learn). In much of my own research, I favor a view that focuses on ways in which teachers' personal histories fundamentally guide their professional learning. I guess that puts me squarely in the second camp, the sociocultural one. I believe that adult learning is about reorienting one's whole self to the world. My view connects nicely with John Dewey's (1916) definition of education: "[Education] is that reconstruction or reorganization of experience which adds to the meaning of experience, and which increases [a person's] ability to direct the course of subsequent experience" (82).

As we think about teacher learning, we should strive to strike an accurate, useful balance. Too much abstraction makes knowledge difficult to apply in one's actual classroom, yet too much contextualization makes knowledge difficult to apply in the face of unpredictable situations, something that all teachers also routinely face. For example, knowing the research on power relations between teachers and students doesn't necessarily help a teacher actually deal with a student who has a problem with authority figures. But *a combination of some research and some reflective practice generally helps teachers to be successful in dealing with the everyday problems they encounter.* Now let's take what we've learned and apply it to a closer look at ourselves and the teacher identity each of us has or is developing.

Focus point

HOW DO TEACHERS LEARN?

Your Interpretive Frame

If we accept that learning emerges out of people's lived contexts and experiences, then it follows that a teacher's knowledge derives from more than intellectual understandings and technical skills. Your teacher knowledge is more than merely the sum of the theories, techniques, and definitions you have learned (or are learning) in your education courses. Instead, your whole self—past, present, and future—is engaged in how you continually understand, enact, evaluate, and refine your teaching practice. In other words, it's not only that some of the *sources* of your professional knowledge are personal in nature, but also that the *process* by which you translate experience into meaning includes both personal and professional factors.

What we might call "teacher development" doesn't reside solely in the abstract, intellectual mind of a teacher. As teachers learn, they make active use of their memories, political and philosophical beliefs, personal dispositions, family experiences, and current and past relationships alongside the professional knowledge and formal educational activities in which they're officially engaged. And whoever they're working with—students, fellow teachers, teacher-education instructors, or peers—is also having an influence on how they are constructing their professional knowledge. Accepting these facts requires us to adopt a broader and deeper way of looking at teacher learning. This is why I prefer the term *identity* instead of *knowledge*, and *teacher-identity development* instead of *teacher learning*. These preferred terms strike me as broader and more holistic and I believe they can help to focus our attention on a fuller range of influences at play in the moment-by-moment activities of teachers in context.

Each of us enters the profession of teaching already armed with deeply embedded ideas about teaching and learning. We have personal reasons why we want to teach; often unexamined beliefs about what it is to be a successful teacher, successful student, or successful parent; hunches about where, as teachers, we will be able to shine and where—conversely—we expect to have trouble in our work; and imagined pictures that we've nurtured for years of what we expect to "look like" as an educator. These embedded ideas and images about teaching and learning form a kind of *interpretive frame* that we rely on, consciously or not, as we learn to teach in some teacher-education program, during our student teaching, and within various internship or professional development networks.

We might hope that any teacher's interpretive frame is altered and improved by his or her teacher-education experience, though it's not always so. Nevertheless, our interpretive frames largely guide us as teachers even after we have finished our preparation programs and find ourselves working with students in schools. Yet, these frames are often hidden from view. Even though they are in active use, they are rarely examined by teachers. A teacher's frame grows out of his general experiences as a human being, and when he begins work as an educator, it also becomes the foundation of his teacher knowledge and therefore represents a fundamental aspect of his professional identity.

TEXTBOX 2.2

Throughout this book, I use the terms *teacher identity* and *professional identity* synonymously.

Perhaps an illustrative metaphor is useful here. Consider a person's general interpretive frame to be like a pair of glasses, as in Photo 2.1.

Pretending that these glasses do not come off, we can probably agree that they would continually and automatically influence the way the world looks to the person who wears them. They're always influencing, ever so slightly or quite a bit, the way the wearer sees things. To extend the metaphor, let's presume that everyone's pair

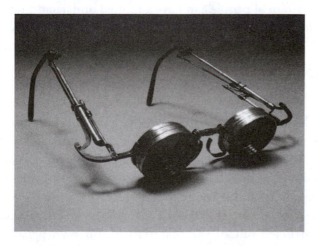

PHOTO 2.1

of glasses is different and invisible, and that each pair emerges out of the person's own biography—his or her own unique mix of lived experiences and human relationships. Philosophically, then, we might say that a kind of moderate subjectivism is at work: rather than assuming one objective social reality, we recognize that there are billions of slightly different, individual views of the world and that these, in the aggregate, become what we call social existence. This isn't to argue for some kind of cultural relativism or philosophical solipsism: there *is* an actual world in place in which many things are not up for debate. The chair I am sitting on is real. The death of innocent people is tragic. Asbestos is toxic.

But the fact remains that many of the nuances of the world are shaded in different hues, ever so slightly, by the interpretive frame of various individuals with whom we come in contact. Everyone's individual existence, and therefore everyone's worldview, is slightly different. There are enough similarities that we can agree on most procedural or declarative knowledge, and can use language in ways understandable by others in our shared cultural communities: a red traffic light means stop; Canada lies to the north of the United States; asking a grocery clerk where the milk is will usually elicit an aisle number or pointed finger.

A group of people can have a mutual understanding of their shared experience as, for example, they discuss a movie they just saw. However, they would probably not all agree in their impressions of that movie. In terms of the deeper subtleties of the world—and many of the things relevant to education!—how the world or movie or classroom looks is slightly different for each person. We could agree on the general plot of the movie we just watched, but we probably *experienced* the movie very differently, and therefore have differing views of its quality, its meaning, and its value to our lives.

For teachers, these pairs of glasses—having been constructed out of the materials of our own personal histories—guide our own education work. They shape decisions we make about which teaching practices we accept and which ones we reject, which kinds of teachers to emulate and which ones to criticize. They shape the image that we have of what a successful classroom would look like—how to arrange the tables or desks; what to put up on the classroom walls; what we picture in our mind's eye when we think of a group of students really chugging along, learning in exciting ways, discovering their own "aha!" moments. They also shape how we interpret and react to our specific teaching contexts: the school, our colleagues, the administration, various policies and reforms. Our glasses color our views of whether we think we're making a difference in the lives of children, whether we believe we can be successful teachers, whether we're enjoying our work. Therefore, they also color how we make career decisions: whether to stay in or leave our present school, whether to continue teaching or consider other kinds of work.

That pair of glasses—that deeply embedded, personal-professional, interpretive frame for teaching—is a double-edged sword. As George Lakoff and Mark Turner (1989) wrote: "Anything that we rely on constantly, unconsciously, and automatically is so much a part of us that it cannot easily be resisted, in large measure because it is rarely even noticed" (63). In a positive way, our embedded interpretive frame acts as a useful personal guide for our professional practice. But in a negative way, it can become a set of biases—a set of personal perspectives developed long ago and then somehow hidden in the shadows of our consciousness even while still actively guiding our views of the world. If we do not unearth, examine, and adjust our interpretive frame as we become teachers, then it controls the kind of teachers we become.

Your Teacher Identity

In my own research I've found that beginning teachers' personal histories shape their professional learning in fundamental ways that are rarely noticed. What I mean by that is that their biography becomes their interpretive frame, shaping not only their general views of the world but also their specific process of becoming a teacher. Much of the recent research I've done has involved investigating these processes and contours of teacher-identity development: how student teachers learn, how teachers' own perspectives shape their work, and how beginning teachers develop into more experienced ones.

What I've consistently found is a complex process of professional learning in which beginning teachers continually combine *professional theories* of teaching from the university (that uppercase Theory) and the *wisdom of practice* from inside the classroom with their own multiple *personal dispositions, conceptions, feelings, goals, and memories* (various lowercase theories) to construct an ever-evolving teaching self. And I've found that this occurs inside *actual contexts of practice*. Schools, universities, and other places where teachers learn carry their own influence on exactly how the participating teacher integrates personal and professional, past and present understandings into teacher knowledge. For example, the school leadership, teaching colleagues, official and unofficial educational policies and norms, and, of course, students and families all factor into the process of a teacher's ongoing identity development. The personal, biographical, nontechnical influences and experiences that each of us possesses sit alongside formal teacher learning and are constantly (as well as automatically and often unconsciously) invoked as we assemble our professional approach to education inside a particular context.

Not only do the interrelated personal and prior influences act as *direct knowledge sources* (for example, I might emphasize poetry in the classroom because my mother loves poetry and over time, because of her, I fell in love with it, too), but they possess an *indirect mediating function* as well. In this indirect way, the personal understandings and dispositions—that pair of glasses from earlier—act as the lens through which I interpret and evaluate the many professional theories and university teaching approaches to which I'm exposed. For example, I might subtly favor university readings or teaching approaches that correspond to how my own teachers taught me, or might reject collaborative learning approaches (even if my university advocates them) because I've personally always disliked working in groups. The point is that, as a beginning teacher, I cannot help but see professional knowledge about teaching and learning through my own personal lens, and so what I think of my formal professional teacher education—how I interpret it, whether I believe it's good or bad, how I will adjust it to fit my predictions for the future—is shaped by the personal views I bring to my teacher learning.

In the end, learning isn't direct and forward-moving; it's not simply internalizing technical or theoretical ideas about teaching and then figuring out how to apply them. Most professional learning in the teachers I have studied was, in fact, indirect and iterative. It was a complex, often automatic process of negotiation and appropriation among many knowledge sources. Teacher learning is actually a looping or spiraling process where one negotiates among different knowledge sources, adapts parts from each of them—or maybe rejects them but is still always evaluating them in relation to each other—and tentatively stitches them together as a way to think about and do teaching. Since this process is continually in motion, a teacher's body of knowledge is constantly changing and growing. To reference a common phrase, a teacher is "always in the act of becoming." And this is true for both the new teacher and the veteran teacher, so it's good to find peace in knowing that you will always be learning to become a better teacher!

Moving from Interpretive Frame to Teacher Identity

That pair of glasses is a metaphor to characterize how any unique individual is shaped by, and goes on to view, the world. I use teacher identity as a term to describe both the *active process* of using personal and professional, past and present influences in order to enact one's teaching and teacher learning, and the *resulting product*: that dynamic assemblage of influences-and-effects (and I connect the words "influences" and "effects" with hyphens to emphasize their interconnectedness) that is always guiding a teacher's perspectives and practices. This tangle of influences-and-effects is akin to what Beijaard et al. (2004) called "a chorus of voices." It shapes how a teacher views himself or herself in relation to the world. And such self-understandings, in turn, guide how the teacher navigates his or her way through the world both personally and professionally.

The world acts on and reacts to the individual person in various ways, and that individual is changed slightly by each of these experiences in the world. In this way, the individual and the larger world engage in a kind of dance with one another—a sometimes clumsy, sometimes perfectly fitting, rarely acknowledged waltz in which the individual is guided by understandings *of* and *for* himself in relation to other people, histories, and contexts. This, I argue, is how we move through the world. Figure 2.1 attempts to graphically illustrate this idea of teacher identity as both process and product, as both the influences on a teacher's knowledge and the effects of those influences. Think of the figure as sets of influence-and-effect ribbons that move and flutter into and out of a dynamic center, constantly changing and being changed by experience and by the influence of the other ribbons. The center is your teacher identity. And the ribbons become filled with the themes of your life—those life experiences that continually shape and reshape you in the flow of everyday practice.

Viewing your learning and your teaching practice through an identity lens allows you to notice the myriad influences on your teaching self—not just the technical, educationally minded ones that our profession empha-

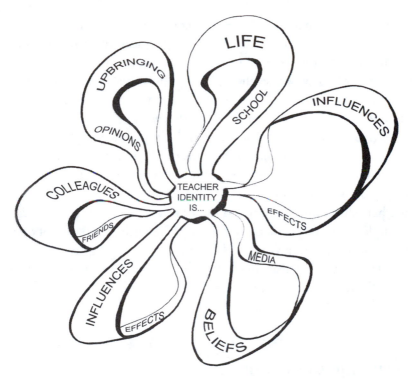

FIGURE 2.1

sizes but all the things that shape you. And it allows you to see that influences on your teacher development are not separate but in fact frequently meld together and interrelate to exert complex influences on your learning. In this way, a teacher-identity focus shows how you are actually relying on dozens of strands of influence that, together, are turning you into the teacher you are becoming. Recognizing, examining, and taking active ownership of all of these strands of influence—and the identity process by which they interrelate—helps you to understand the teacher you are becoming.

CONCLUSION

Thus far I've been discussing teacher identity as a rather abstract concept rather than as something concrete and clear. I have begun with foundational discussions in order to clarify why it is important for you to consider your teacher identity and how it fits in with and relates to existing educational theories and topics. But it would be helpful at this point to have a more grounded, real-life example of what teacher identity looks like in practice and how it works to shape an actual teacher's learning. If it's going to be useful, one's teacher identity must be fairly easy to recognize and understand. A real example of teacher identity in practice might help us to see how a person's own biography ends up shaping teacher development. And it could highlight the multiple ways in which a teacher as whole person is actively implicated in her decisions to accept or reject her teacher-education program and in her ways of becoming a teacher.

The following chapter takes up this task. Presenting the story of one student teacher in the process of becoming a beginning teacher, the chapter frames teacher learning as a complex, iterative, personalized journey of teacher identity construction.

DISCUSSION QUESTIONS

1. Are you someone who has difficulty with or experiences frustration when reading educational theory or published research? Why do you think that is so? What strategies might you employ in order to find useful ways to engage with academic theory and research texts?

2. What theories were (or are) emphasized in your teacher-education program? How do these compare with the ideas presented in this chapter?

3. How do your views of learning influence your current teaching practices? Can you think of concrete ways to adjust your teaching so it's better aligned with your beliefs about how people learn?

4. Do you regularly engage in conversations with colleagues and peers about theory? If not, how can you instigate conversation around theories of learning, teaching, and teacher development?

FURTHER READING

Fosnot, C., ed. 2005. *Constructivism*. New York: Teachers College Press.

Lave, J., and E. Wenger. 1991. *Situated Learning*. Cambridge: Cambridge University Press.

Oakes, J., and M. Lipton. 2006. *Teaching to Change the World*, 3rd ed. New York: McGraw Hill.

Olsen, B. 2010. "'I Am Large, I Contain Multitudes': Teacher Identity as Useful Frame for Research, Practice, and Diversity in Education." In A. Ball and C. Tyson, eds., *The American Educational Research Association Handbook on Studying Diversity in Teacher Education*. Lanham, MD: Rowman and Littlefield.

CHAPTER THREE

COMBINING THE PERSONAL AND THE PROFESSIONAL IN TEACHING

An Example

LIZ: One of the things I've noticed that's made me not so thrilled with teaching is that I don't really like my behavior.

BRAD: What do you mean?

LIZ: I'm doing the things I never thought I'd do.

BRAD: Like what?

LIZ: Just the way I react to kids, the things that piss me off. Getting kind of, you know, snotty with kids. . . . When I get angry with a class it's because I'm trying to hold them to a particular tautness, and they won't—it won't work. Because it's my feeling that for kids to be on task they need to be on task, need order. They need to be focused. And it's my job to keep them focused. When I can't keep a class focused, or when those kids refuse, I can pull, and I can pull in as hard as I want, but I'm going to break the string before they get it. Before they straighten up. And so I had to make a decision: Am I going to keep pulling and kicking kids out and having, you

know, what could be mutiny—and what's *been* mutiny?
Or do I try and relax a little bit and hope for as much as
I can get?

—Liz, a first-year California
high-school English teacher

I HAVE ARGUED THAT IT IS paramount for every
teacher to reflect on his or her own teacher identity,
and I have offered a theoretical justification for adopting a teacher-identity framework. In this chapter I will
demonstrate what teacher identity actually looks like
and, in doing so, narrate some of the early struggles associated with becoming a teacher. More specifically, I will
use the concept of teacher identity to illuminate how
hard it can be for a new teacher to reconcile his or her
prior and personal experiences with the more professional, technical aspects of teacher education. Acknowledging all the influences on one's teacher learning often
requires the teacher to confront multiple personal and
professional conflicts. And, although these conflicts over
time give the teacher newer and richer views of himself
or herself as a teacher, while he or she is in the process of
recognizing and working through them they can cause
frustration and anguish. Such is the challenge of early-career teacher development. Even the most amazing veteran teachers had to go through it in order to become
amazing.

In the late 1990s I spent two years observing, talking
with, and learning from Liz as she became a high-school
English teacher in California. Our first year together was
during her teacher-education program in a large public
university's one-year graduate program; our second year
together was her first year as an English teacher working
at the same California school in which she student-taught
the year before. Like any teacher—like any person—Liz
herself was a complex bundle of influences, beliefs, values,
features, and perceptions. This bundle of pieces, what we

might call a "self," appeared on the surface to be categorizable: Liz, a white woman from a middle-class background in Staten Island, New York, was in her late twenties, college-educated, confident, idealistic, able to crack a joke, naturally self-deprecating, the daughter of two teachers, and someone who loved rock music. Educational researchers might cast her as the typical teacher candidate (Calderhead 1988; Wideen et al. 1998). Yet, as I came to know Liz—analyzing her ways of teaching, thinking, talking, and acting—I found that she was, of course, unique, clearly possessing her own distinctive teacher identity.

Some of you may readily identify with details of Liz's story, and even those of you who do not should benefit from the chance to hear that story. You will better understand the concept of teacher identity by way of a grounded example. Either way, by illuminating teacher identity as a concrete, visible process, I will use this chapter to set up the second half of the book: once you understand what teacher identity is and how it shapes teacher learning and practice, then you're ready to attend to your own teacher identity.

Liz's beginning teacher development was largely a story of Liz fashioning a professional teaching identity out of a mix of the facts of her personal history, what she was learning in her teacher-education program, and what she experienced during her first two years in the classroom. As Liz tried to assemble a useful bundle of understandings about teaching and learning, she was weaving together myriad influences into something she considered coherent: something that she believed worked for her. Liz was constructing her teacher identity (although I don't think she realized it at the time, and she wouldn't have used that terminology). She had to reconcile competing beliefs about what a teacher is; she had to address the power that her own biography had over her; she had to integrate her university's ideas about education with

The value of framing Liz's professional development in terms of *teacher identity* is that it acknowledges and celebrates her uniqueness.

other teaching influences from her life; and she had to figure out how to learn from her students at the same time she was teaching them. It was hard work and often emotionally taxing, but she felt driven to succeed.

One important lesson from Liz's experience is a painful one: she was offered very little professional support in recognizing and navigating her teacher-identity conflicts. Neither her education program nor her mentors pointed out how interrelated, deep, and emotionally taxing the process of becoming a teacher can be. No one talked to her about teacher learning in terms of identity changes. No one helped her understand that becoming a teacher is full of contradictions, that conflicts are resolved slowly, that a person's teacher identity changes and grows over time—in short, that she needn't always be so hard on herself. It's a difficult process, but, over time, it gives way to insight, wisdom, and a successful, newly developed professional identity.

The value of framing Liz's professional development in terms of *teacher identity* is that it acknowledges and celebrates her uniqueness; Liz brings characteristics, experiences, and talents together in a way that no one else does. But a teacher-identity frame also highlights the commonalities inherent in becoming a teacher. Liz may be unique, but the contours of her beginning teacher development are shared by many early-career teachers. Yes, the details may be specific to Liz, but the larger patterns, complexities, and contradictions are probably common to many. I suspect that learning about Liz's experience will allow you to reflect on parts of your own. Her story teaches us that the initial tensions and emotional conflicts of teaching are common (you're not alone!); that growth happens . . . but incrementally (be patient!); and that the more a teacher examines his or her identity processes, the more successful he or she will become (be self-reflective!). Liz learned through her experience, and I share this narrative with you so that you may learn something about yourself as you embark on a similar journey.

Liz's Tug-of-War between Student-Centered and Teacher-Centered Models of Teaching

As I studied Liz for two years while she was learning to teach, it became clear to me that her process of development was largely about constructing a teacher identity by considering and experimenting with several models of teaching:

- The *teacher-as-cool-friend* model of her own "hippest, jeans-wearing English teacher" in tenth grade, on whom she "had a crush."
- The *teacher-as-expert* model of her English-teacher father, who "believed in kids sitting in rows facing the teacher" and was "flabbergasted" that Liz's credentialing program employed group learning: "But why are you paying tuition to listen to the kid next to you? He doesn't know any more than you do. It's the professor you're paying for."
- The *student-centered/cooperative learning teacher* model her credentialing program espoused—"It's the emerging paradigm," one of her professors told me, but Liz wasn't so sure.
- The *teacher-as-technician* model that her favorite teacher-education professor embodied and advocated: "Her stuff is so concrete and useful," Liz said to me.
- The *teacher-as-agent-of-social-change* model that Liz's family instilled in her: "[Teaching] was this noble thing to do in our family," she reported.

So, while Liz was struggling with the day-to-day challenges of being a new teacher, she was also constantly managing which of these five teacher types she felt she should be for herself, for her students, and for others. Her sometimes conscious, sometimes automatic manipulation of these models of teaching made use of the literally dozens of strands of influence on her teacher-identity development. Liz was organizing, evaluating, adjusting, and fitting together knowledge from diverse sources—personal and professional, past and current—into a body of understandings of what it meant for her to be a teacher.

In order to illustrate this process, I present one central issue that characterized Liz's development: her ongoing struggle with the competing models of teaching as *student-centered* or as *teacher-centered*. This involves a century-long debate between constructivism and didactic instruction (see Textbox 3.1), and it figured prominently in Liz's teacher-identity development.

PHASE ONE: LIZ ENTERS HER CREDENTIALING PROGRAM

I had an argument this weekend with my father, who's been an English teacher for thirty-five years. He asked what kinds of things I'm learning [in my university program]. I explained that the teaching models we're learning are very different from the way he teaches. I told him that we're learning to privilege the student over the teacher, that teaching now is child-centered. This elicited pretty much the response I expected from him: "You'll learn that none of that works. Group work is nice in the textbook but it's impossible in the classroom." You see, my father believes in kids sitting in rows or perhaps in a horseshoe; in either form they face the teacher. My father believes that the teacher has the information. That's why he's the teacher. Groups may make kids less shy, more expressive, but inevitably they collapse into social discussions. What's worse, he says, they don't prepare kids for what they'll see in college.

—Liz

By the end of the first month of her teacher-preparation program, Liz had decided that student-centered

TEXTBOX 3.1   THE STUDENT-CENTERED VERSUS TEACHER-CENTERED CONTINUUM

For more than a century, the tension between these two paradigms has endured. Indeed, it has factored into almost every debate in education for succeeding generations, including the debate over the value of lecturing versus group work, the discussion about phonics versus the whole-language approach to reading, and work on the relative merits of computer-aided instruction, among other issues.

On the *student-centered* side, developmentalists, humanists, and constructivists emphasize the student as the center of the curriculum and argue that a teacher should discover each individual child's own "urgent impulses and habits," and then, by supplying the proper environment and encouragement, direct students "in a fruitful and orderly way" toward self-discovery (Kliebard 1995). The motivation for learning, it is argued, will take care of itself.

On the *teacher-centered*—or *traditional* or *didactic*—side of the debate, social-efficiency theorists and direct-instruction advocates believe that any group of students should be taught mostly in the same way and to the same extent (anything less is inequitable); they place emphasis on the teacher delivering standardized information to students (often in lectures) and leading them in drills to reinforce internalization of that information (Kliebard 1995).

Of course, in practice the debate is rarely as polarized or simple as this summary pretends. Most educators conceive of this tension as a broad space in which effective practice lies somewhere in between the extremes, and caveats and contradictions abound. But Liz didn't know this, and—as we'll soon see—her teacher-education program did not help her to make sense of it.

teaching and teacher-centered teaching existed at opposite poles of a continuum, and that to lean in one direction necessarily sacrificed the other. She framed it as a tug-of-war between the two sides. Much of her prior understanding of teaching had come from her father, and when she spoke of her father's teaching, she often employed the language of the teacher-as-expert model: a conception that Liz set in direct opposition to the student-centered model she believed represented her university program's ideal. She found it difficult to reconcile for herself these two views of teaching.

Her father had just retired after teaching English for thirty-five years in several New York City public and private high schools. Liz told me that her dad had always loved teaching and considered himself to be good at it; he was known and respected in the field and had published a grammar book. Discussing her father as a teacher, she tended to use terms reflecting a cluster of teaching models: the traditional teacher, the teacher as expert, the teacher who succeeds primarily with academically motivated students (and disappoints the remainder), and the satisfied professional at the end of a successful career. Liz told me:

> And you know, thinking about it now, or recently as I have, you know, my dad was a good teacher. And he seemed always to have been a good teacher. . . . He stuck to the text . . . students were able to understand [and] enjoy things that they read. I think he was very good in discussion, kind of doing that switchback with students like, "What did you mean by . . . ?" And making good insights on the fly, which is something I hope to get better at. I think the thing is, that he enjoyed it. You know, I think when you're good at something it's fun to do. He liked it.

Here, Liz was conceiving of effective teaching as (1) adhering closely to the text, (2) having students enjoy what they read, (3) fashioning discussions that draw on student comments, (4) making good insights on the fly, and—most interesting—(5) finding fun in it, because, "when you're good at something it's fun to do." These are powerful teaching attributes, and ones that Liz held with her throughout our two years together and frequently demonstrated in her teaching. They were therefore not only descriptions of her father's practice but also influences on her own.

Liz's university credentialing program, however, advocated a very different model. It put forward a student-centered approach to teaching that emphasized cooperative learning, students constructing their own meanings of the material, and a rejection of both lecturing and the belief that listening is learning. Given the influence of her father and her own largely traditional schooling experiences, Liz was initially skeptical of these cooperative learning and process approaches, even though her professors favored them:

> I don't know if the group work thing is good. . . . I don't think it's the best way to teach. I like to feel that the person in charge is an expert in her subject. It's kind and empowering of the expert to say, "Well, what do you think?" That makes me feel strong and intelligent, and yet, I'd rather have the benefit of her expertise on the subject.

Notice that she is basically ventriloquizing her dad's view as her own here. Liz was concerned that, in its desire to push student-centered teaching, her program's approach failed to recognize any value whatsoever in traditional methods of teaching.

Additionally, like many new teachers, Liz was implicitly favoring concrete approaches over abstract perspectives. Though both models—student-centered and teaching-centered—offered specific instructional methods, the fact that her program wrapped its teaching methods inside theoretical perspectives and academic articles might have made them seem less palatable than the "this-is-what-works" immediacy that commonly marks the way practicing teachers talk, and that characterized her father's remarks about teaching. At least she *knew* her father's approach had worked for him. Her program was still, to her, just Theory.

Yet, when Liz began talking about the particulars of her father's curricular and pedagogical approaches, she acknowledged that his didactic, teacher-centered methods were not wholly sufficient either. She understood that her program's approach—being newer, ostensibly better researched, focused on the learner instead of the teacher, and legitimized by virtue of its university status—should be taken seriously. She knew that it would take time for her to figure it out and really learn to do it well, but that didn't make it any easier as she went to school each day. And she felt anxious that her program was expecting such a sudden, total identity shift. In the flow of her teacher learning, it was easier to rely on what she knew—even if it contradicted her professors—than to take on an unfamiliar view of teaching and learning.

The tug-of-war continued and, a month or two into her program, Liz wanted to decrease the level of anxiety she was feeling. She believed the situation required an either/or decision: that adopting one meant rejecting the other. She was "trying on" both her dad's methods and her program's philosophies to decide which one felt more reasonable. She felt that she was being pulled in two directions, and that neither side acknowledged any validity to the other. She interpreted her program's preferred pedagogy as mostly having students work in groups, share their own understandings with each other in discussions, and make use of a teacher who, in her words, "facilitates" and "scoots [students] around so they hit the right places." However, because of her dad she strongly believed that the teacher—as the disciplinary expert—had an obligation to deliver content to students, who would learn from the teacher's knowledge. She viewed acceptance of the student-centered model as a rejection of the teacher-as-expert model and therefore as a rejection of her father-as-model.

Further complicating Liz's dilemma were the personal feelings she had come to have about two of her three primary university instructors. Liz did not much care for either her seminar leader or her curriculum and instruction professor, and her personal, emotional reactions to these instructors affected her view of the professional ideas they advocated.

I've found that such a situation is typical, and it highlights the interconnected roles of emotions and interpersonal relationships in teacher learning. For example, during a first-semester curriculum and instruction class meeting, Liz felt personally attacked by the instructor for defending a traditional, lecture-based teacher that the group had read about the previous week. Liz had raised her hand and announced that she did not think all lecturing was bad, that there was value in some of the teaching methods typically ascribed to "traditional" teachers, and that this teacher was getting an unfair rap in the class. The professor became visibly annoyed and publicly disagreed with Liz. After class, in the hallway, Liz said to me: "She scowled at me. Did you see that? I'll never bring up that again. I sure wouldn't want to offend her," and at this Liz rolled her eyes in sarcasm and frustration. Liz spoke negatively of this professor for the rest of the year and disengaged from the course discussions and material.

I can sympathize with Liz's struggles. As she was becoming a teacher, she was being required to choose among competing models of teaching—and attached to those models were real people, real emotions, and deeply personal memories of her own experiences in classrooms. Those on each side of the debate were unforgiving of the opposing side; no one was talking with Liz about the contradictions and emotional difficulties associated with the kind of identity work that was occurring. Liz would have benefited from honest, straightforward conversations about the identity conflicts, emotional roller-coaster rides, and myriad contradictions involved in authentically and deeply "becoming a teacher."

PHASE TWO: LIZ DIGS DEEPER INTO THE TENSION

By the end of her first semester in her preparation program, Liz had begun teasing out the complexities of why she was simultaneously drawn to, and skeptical of, each of the two teaching approaches. She had begun considering the tug-of-war in more nuanced ways. She was also feeling pressure to make up her mind somehow; she was only weeks away from her student-teaching practicum. It was fast becoming very real.

She was reluctant to abandon the notion of teacher-as-expert, believing that to do so would mean that only the students were experts; she felt this meant that students would simply share their own half-baked opinions, and that didn't seem right to her. She agreed with her father that group work was a cumbersome, inefficient approach that often devolved into students chatting. Yet, she began for the first time to acknowledge the problems inherent in his traditional approach and started to see some of the logic of her program's student-centered view. Liz was beginning to reject parts of each, to accept other parts, and to think more deeply about the kind of teacher she hoped to be. *In fact, she had effected a significant shift: instead of seeing the two approaches as mutually exclusive, she was beginning to consider how to assemble a hybrid of both.*

Focus point

Though I'm oversimplifying it here, multiple strands of her personal history were being invoked, reassessed, and employed as active influences in what was an ongoing construction of her teacher identity. Specifically, the process was being deepened by reflecting on *the opinions of her girlfriend, memories of her own school experiences and, in particular, a favorite tenth-grade teacher*, and *her political and moral reasons for teaching*. These influences deepened Liz's teacher-identity development because recognition of them pushed her to reevaluate her father's teaching and clarify her own interpretation of her program's model—and they provided additional teaching models to consider. The process wasn't easy, but she was clearly making progress. For her, a large part of the challenge was being honest with herself about her father as a teaching influence:

> LIZ: It's interesting finding out now and taking classes now and seeing the new age of teaching and comparing it to the way my dad has taught for the last thirty-five years and getting real disillusioned with my dad as a teacher.
>
> BRAD: Why?
>
> LIZ: I've seen his lesson plans. I've seen the essays and grades, and I know what he looks for. And it's like a reality check. In some ways I'm finding out my dad wasn't the greatest teacher. What my dad is really good at is teaching the smart classes. I think the kids who really need it fall to the back of the room, and that's a way that my dad is not a great teacher. My brother who's in his early thirties now has friends who are his own age who were my dad's students. One is bright [and liked my dad as a teacher]. And another is like, "Oh, your dad's Mr. Mason? He made me feel like I was nothing." She became an expert in repairing airplanes and writes manuals on how to repair airplanes. But my dad made her feel like she couldn't do anything. I want to teach for people like her too.

Liz's girlfriend was encouraging her to think about who loses in a teacher-as-didactic-expert approach like her father's:

> I talk to my girlfriend a bit about it. Partly because I know how much she hated school as a kid. For her school was a big problem, and it's important for me to hear that. My girlfriend has taught me: "Okay, when

that kid comes in late after lunch every day and passes notes, don't yell at her. She might be struggling." I know how much [my girlfriend's] insecurities about her language abilities and grammar and her ability to be articulate were just like a cloud over her. I don't know what happened, but for some reason that wasn't good. So, I definitely have that in mind now, to keep an eye on that. Understanding that has really made me less of an elitist, to see that and to respect someone who's like that. And I think I'll bring that into the classroom in a way that I don't think I would have a few months ago.

Key concept Stephen Krashen's *affective filter*

From her girlfriend, Liz gained a professional understanding that, as the teacher, she must never make a student insecure over his or her language difficulties. What Liz describes as a "cloud over her" is what linguist Stephen Krashen (1987) would call the *affective filter*, but no matter the terminology, Liz believed that to engage in this kind of emotional bullying constituted teacher "elitism." Stephen Krashen's **affective filter** is a barrier that prevents people from learning because they are tense, angry, or otherwise emotionally uncomfortable. Liz was realizing that a student's levels of anxiety and self-esteem are related to motivation and therefore will affect learning. This was a powerful lesson that emerged from integrating her girlfriend's advice with her own deepening views of her father's teaching, and a reevaluation of her program's teaching philosophy.

Liz also reconsidered her own secondary-school experiences:

In my own experiences in high school, group work—the kind of collaborative learning or student-centered thing—was never big. It was more about sitting in your chair facing the teacher for fifty minutes until the bell rang. Either you wrote or you read, or the teacher told you stuff that you were supposed to write down. But that's not what school is anymore. And in part I'm glad it's not that anymore, but it makes it much more difficult on the teacher.

Academically, Liz had done relatively well in junior-high and high-school English. She mostly attributed this success to her English-teacher parents:

> I was a lazy student. My parents were English teachers, so somehow I got by on just having a well-trained ear. I knew, for the most part, what sounded right. I was in the smart class all through junior high school. . . . I cheated a bit. I discovered that if I asked my parents general questions about [Shakespeare plays, for example], I'd leave the dinner table with specific answers, interpretations, and insights. All I had to do was remember them long enough to repeat them in class the next day.

Although Liz got by academically, however, she was neither learning nor happy:

> I never felt I was taught vocabulary in any meaningful way in high school. . . . I think that if I had had fun and satisfying experiences with vocabulary words in high school, I might have had more facility and comfort with speaking, reading, and writing than I had during and after high school.

Five times (twice in conversation with me, three times in writing assignments for her program) she recounted a story of hating school, of feeling that she did not fit in and that her ideas were not being validated, until she came across her tenth-grade English teacher. Liz remembers feeling disenfranchised by the school community that she was a part of: it (and the traditional teaching that characterized it) made her feel unwanted and unfulfilled. And Liz credits one particular teacher with turning things around for her. It was her own high-school teacher that evidently opened up the world of academics for her.

As I talked with Liz, I learned that Liz's own English teacher was becoming her professional role model. This influence arose as Liz began to reflect deeply on her own experiences in high-school English:

> I never completed a book until I was a sophomore in high school. Finally, I had an English teacher who was fun and funny. For her, I wanted to read. Thinking back, I probably just had a crush on her and wanted to prove my intellectual worth. But at least I read. For the first time, reading didn't feel like a chore. I had insights of my own to share in class. From that year on, I was a reader. I became an Honors English student. I read novels for school and for fun.

A week later, as we were talking about why she wanted to be a teacher, she returned to this time in her past. After first referencing her dad, she began to talk again about her own high-school experiences:

> I didn't like school when I was a kid. And that's unfortunate. . . . But during my sophomore year I had this teacher who was the hippest, jeans-wearing English teacher. She was tough and funny and inspired insight and expression in everyone that I didn't feel I got from other teachers.
>
> BRAD: What did she do that made the environment such that this occurred?
>
> LIZ: She was funny . . . and it was a lot about the thing a teacher does when they're waiting to say the thing they're thinking: "Okay. Good. And let's see if somebody else can come up with the right answer. Good, Jimmy." . . . She may have had a right answer in her head, but she wasn't overbearing about it. . . . She made me feel smart by letting us come up with the answers.

Liz clearly considered having this teacher to be a pivotal point not only in her own schooling trajectory but also in her decision to teach. This teaching model—teacher as hip, jeans-wearing, fun person who makes students feel that their contributions are valued—emerged from Liz's personal history with school. In addition, it appears that, as in the situation where the animosity she felt toward two of her university professors had such an impact, Liz's personal feelings for a teacher had become inextricably entangled with the professional model the teacher represented, but this time it was the mirror image of her relationship with the teacher-education instructors. (And it might not be coincidental that Liz often wore denim pants when teaching, even though her seminar leader strongly discouraged it!)

The link between her admiration and respect for the teacher, on the one hand, and her motivation to work hard in that class, on the other, shaped Liz's subsequent conception of an ideal teacher. Liz believed for herself that a teacher who is liked by students has an additional motivational tool at her disposal. In a later interview, I asked Liz what qualities she felt a successful English teacher needed to possess, and she began describing, almost verbatim, qualities she had used months earlier to describe her tenth-grade teacher. Eventually, I asked, "So, is it fair to say you want to be your own tenth-grade English teacher?" She laughed and agreed. And, finally, memories of this experience offered Liz a ready-made model of successful teacher as hip friend who attends to students' needs to have their ideas validated in class—a counterbalance, in some ways, to what she found disappointing in her father.

Another influence on Liz's professional identity emerged when she returned to her reasons for entering teaching, more specifically to her belief that teaching is a political act:

Why do I want to teach? I saw that there was a need. People were not getting educated in high school. So the population that I've become interested in is the at-risk, whatever that means. The kids who need to know how to write a cover letter or a resume. The people who are not taken seriously in society because they can't communicate seriously using academic English. . . . [W]hile we're so concerned with social inequality and economic reality and crime and all the complaints in our country, it seems ironic to deny these populations the best education they can have. That's when it occurred to me that teaching might be a good direction to go in.

Liz's moral/political concerns for students in a democratic society and her reasons for entering teaching acted as a significant influence on her teaching. In fact, one's reasons for entering the profession have a lot to do with the kind of teacher one becomes (Olsen 2008b). In Liz's case, reflecting on her political reasons for teaching deepened her views about the teacher-centered versus student-centered tug-of-war she was experiencing. As she recognized who got left out of her father's approach against the student population she hoped to serve, she concluded that her dad's model might not be the best one for her purposes. Liz intended to teach a different student population, a student population with more diversity and more learning challenges, and one that reflected the changing world around her. Her dad's teaching might be primarily a professional or academic endeavor (in her opinion), but she considered hers a political act, too.

However, employing the model of the teacher as an agent of social change didn't offer Liz a way out of the student-centered versus teacher-centered conflict; it only deepened the existing dilemma. She felt that student-centered teaching—while admirably focusing on students' comfort levels, their own construction of learning, and the power of students learning from each other—was neither rigorous nor content-based enough to truly give "at-risk" students the education they needed for societal success. Viewing teaching through a social-justice

One's reasons for entering the profession have a lot to do with the kind of teacher one becomes.

lens, she admired the traditional model's strict insistence on students learning academic skills and on students having access to an expert's content knowledge. She saw a political importance to ensuring that historically underserved students learn those skills and content that she believed would allow them inside the arena of middle-class success. In several interview passages, she acknowledged that standard English might be a culturally loaded language, but its mastery was necessary:

> [Standard English] is not value free. I mean, maybe it's elitist in its construction or who gets to create it and who gets to decide what is and is not acceptable. Fine. It is. But that's not the issue I need to deal with now. The issue I need to deal with is how I can give students the most power. And power comes from them knowing the language of those who hold the power.

She felt strongly that historically underserved students needed access to the rules and codes of the English language if they were going to succeed in the United States. It therefore concerned her that the student-centered model that her credentialing program advocated seemed to lower expectations in order to make students comfortable:

> We're waiting for kids to feel comfortable with learning, and in the meantime they don't know the difference between a subject and a verb and can't construct a sentence, which means they can't communicate outside the classroom. I think it's very important for kids to understand that proper English is the standard code, and is valuable.

Yet, she simultaneously feared that traditional, didactic teaching, in its rigidity and its emphasis on product (not process) and transferable knowledge (not student understandings), precluded many students, especially those she expected to teach, from feeling comfortable with learning. Like her girlfriend who was made to feel insecure about the things she didn't know, Liz appreciated student-centered teaching for accepting that a student's emotional comfort correlates to learning. She was also warming up to the idea of students constructing their own knowledge. Liz wanted to adopt a version of the student-centered model of teaching, but she didn't believe that her credentialing program was offering her the right way to do it. She also was unwilling to drop all of the more traditional, teacher-as-disciplinary-expert model that her father represented. With this struggle, this set of conflicting teacher models, this in-flux professional identity, Liz began her student teaching. Grappling with these contradictions would be worked into the process of her imminent classroom experience on a daily basis.

PHASE THREE: LIZ TEACHES

Liz conducted her student teaching practicum from January until June at a midsized, mostly urban, public high school in California. Because the school employed a block schedule, Liz taught two ninety-minute periods of English five days a week. In June, she was offered a full-time position for the next year, which she accepted. Liz's year and a half of teaching experience generated a new—and very immediate—source of professional knowledge that furthered her teacher-identity development. Once a beginning teacher enters the classroom, previous ideals and notions of teaching suddenly change, blend, and shift during the daily process of working directly with students in the school setting. But answers to previous dilemmas aren't necessarily found that quickly.

Liz found that teaching was more difficult than she had expected, and her views of students changed, too. She felt frustrated that students respected neither the classroom norms she set nor the lessons she put forward; in fact, she felt that they took advantage of her student-centered attention to them. Liz had first believed strongly in individual student agency, telling me halfway through her first semester of her credentialing program that "the responsibility to perform always falls directly on the student," but now she began to soften this view. By the end of January, she said, "The motivating factor for a student's ability or inability to perform may certainly fall outside his control. I'm taking into consideration where he's coming from, but certainly he's the one that has to perform." Liz began positing more and more external factors affecting student success; she began to consider that their experiences in immigrant families made a fundamental difference:

> I know that for me, you know, my parents made sure I was in line, that I did the work I needed to do. They'd find out if I wasn't doing my homework. I'd get yelled at. I don't know that that's the kind of guidance that all these kids are getting when 60 percent of that school is an immigrant population. I certainly think that poor immigrant families have a lot more on their minds to deal with, with their families, than sitting over their kids' shoulders to make sure they're doing their homework.

Notice how Liz still viewed teaching and her students through her own personal experience, but now she was beginning to differentiate between her family and their families and the kinds of experiences they would have had that were different.

As she became familiar with her students, she came to believe that because their backgrounds were different from her own, she had to find new ways to connect with them. She couldn't be the teacher who would have connected best with herself when she was their age. Her students weren't multiple copies of herself; she began to realize that she would have to become the teacher *they* needed her to be, not the teacher she had always thought she would be. It was an important step in her identity development for her to realize that their needs would have to dictate what kind of teacher she would be.

She found the quality of students' skills—their writing, speaking, homework, and intellectual analysis—surprisingly low. To explain this vast distance between their skills and her expectations, she first looked to the students themselves and blamed them for their failings: they weren't working hard enough; they were unwilling to accept that schooling is important for their own success. But soon she began to locate the blame in society instead. She placed some responsibility on the students and their parents, but gently and only indirectly, because she viewed the families and children as being shaped by larger forces of social discrimination and disadvantage. The low skills and motivation of the students were not their fault, she reasoned, and not her fault, but rather the fault of the system.

Observing her teach, I saw many places where her particular view of student efficacy—a fragile mix of student agency and student powerlessness—emerged in the classroom. It seemed that she made adjustments to her teaching to lower her own emotional fatigue of expecting too much from herself and from them. She now allowed students to choose not to read aloud if they wished (they could say "pass"); at the end of silent, sustained reading, she no longer asked students to describe their books to the class. One day I asked her if she knew that during silent, sustained reading, the boy next to me simply looked at the back cover of an atlas for twenty minutes:

> Yeah, I don't care. . . . It doesn't really matter to me what they're reading as long as there's something that they're looking at. [One student] has been looking at a legal writing book for, like, a week or two weeks. She says she wants to be a lawyer. You know, I don't know if she understands it or not. Probably not. But there's something she's drawn to in it. So I'm fine with that.

Some days she treated students as if they had significant agency over their actions and learning. She would tell them that the onus of succeeding in school, and in life, fell on each of them. Other days she would attribute student failure to a lack of support from family, from the school culture, from society—conceiving of students as products of larger forces. Interestingly, though, she always attributed their *successes* solely to themselves. ("He's just so smart." "She works hard." "Because he's more mature than the others.") It appears that her compassion for her students created an inherent reluctance to blame them for failure yet an instant willingness to credit them for success—perhaps a logical incongruence but a nicely optimistic, child-centered equilibrium. Trying to make sense of her own teacher development, she had built a fragile, temporary mix of individual agency and structural determinism—a teacher-identity balance that allowed her to believe she was making a difference in the face of difficult circumstances.

PHASE FOUR: LIZ FINISHES HER SECOND YEAR

Near the end of her first year of full-time teaching, our second year together, I observed Liz for two consecutive days, and then we talked in her classroom for two tape-recorded hours. This snapshot (in a scene that is, of course, forever in progress) of her teacher development revealed that in some ways Liz's initial views about teaching had changed, and in other ways they had deepened. Both aspects seemed to cause her some anguish and revealed the uncomfortable reality that the development of one's teacher identity never ends.

Her ideas about her father's teaching model had developed but had not dramatically changed. Liz concluded that her dad was a good teacher, but with two important provisos that allowed her to retain pieces of his model while simultaneously rejecting its philosophical core.

First, she decided that he was an effective teacher only for
"higher-end," older students—those juniors and seniors
who worked hard, succeeded often, and could learn from a
teacher who primarily talked about literature and writing
and challenged students to think hard and write well.
("[His students were okay with] this kind of very traditional, old-school kind of setting . . . fifty-minute periods
and discussion then reading then lecture. You know, your
basic stuff. . . . [But] I couldn't pull it off.") She concluded
that these students could more or less teach themselves;
they needed her father primarily as someone who would
provide interesting insights and an intellectual environment. This type of student still existed, but she was more
interested in the many others who would never thrive under this model.

Yet, she also believed that there were components of her
dad's traditional model that she could employ. Instead of
experiencing a tug-of-war between her dad's approach and
her program's philosophy, she now embraced a hybridiza-
tion of teacher-centered and student-centered instructional approaches. She began to believe that she did not
have to *replace* progressivist approaches with her father's
traditional methods (or vice versa); instead, she could *sup-
plement* the progressivist approaches with elements from
her dad's model. Thus, she would stand at the front of the
room and offer expert interpretations of the text, yet also
implement student-centered activities and remain sensitive to student attitudes and interpretations.

I observed as Liz taught a ninth-grade lesson on the
beginning scenes of *Romeo and Juliet* that attempted
just this kind of blend. She created a lecturing structure
that employed the external framework of a teacher
monologue—teacher informs students of textual meanings, connections, and contexts—while inside it facilitating a back-and-forth, student-centered conversation
where she asked questions, listened to responses, and
tried to weave student comments into her own comments. She took this dialogue-within-a-monologue

where she wanted it to go, but attempted to use student answers and comments to arrive there. This student conversation wrapped inside a teacher lecture emerged as the linguistic structure Liz favored.

Second, she finally accepted that her father's model succeeded in large part because he had had decades of practice: "I now think it may have been easier [for him], or looked easier, because he had been doing it for so long before I showed up." Entering teaching, Liz had initially believed she would immediately be ready to be a perfect teacher; she had conceived of teaching—owing to her many, often personal sources of knowledge—as merely knowing one's subject, being thoughtful, remembering one's own past, and respecting all students. This entering disposition led her to believe that she would teach well right out of the gate. However, she found the situation to be otherwise and had to reconceive her ideas about teaching. Now, for her, effective teaching required a deep intuition about students and proper pacing, a masterful ability to explain concepts and "make good insights on the fly," a patience that results from confidence, and a firmer hand with discipline. Interestingly, though, she believed these characteristics came from experience—not further or better training. She still believed her program had not taught her much that was useful.

In addition, Liz had initially believed that an effective teacher must be expert in his or her subject (a belief deriving from her father's model): "Sometimes I feel like a bit of a fraud. I mean I graduated with an English degree . . . but the list of books I have completed is unbelievably short. I feel like a phony—that I'll be found out one of these days." Yet, by the end of her first year, she had changed that view, now concluding that subject expertise emerges with experience and that she shouldn't feel bad for not yet knowing her subject well. During her second year, she told me that "being competent" is enough, and she acknowledged that because of time constraints she sometimes merely skimmed through the reading assignment the night before.

She concluded that she would learn by reflecting on and improving her own classroom practice, not by adhering more closely to the knowledge and practices that her program had stressed.

By the end of our two years together, Liz had built a tentative, beginning teacher identity in which neither side (the traditional models from her past or the progressivist ones from her program) felt fully comfortable to her. And she found that her hybrid of the two models didn't work, either. Since her program appeared not to acknowledge or support her through this personal-professional angst in her teacher-identity process, she often felt alone and confused as a teacher. Over time, Liz will undoubtedly find her professional footing. And yet, if she had been offered an explicit, supportive, honest view of these competing, sometimes contradictory facets of her teacher-identity development, she would have experienced less anxiety and less confusion and could have more easily constructed teaching approaches that worked for her and her students. Instead, she was left to carry out these tasks mostly by herself.

Finally, her initial reasons for entry into the profession now appeared distant, and this saddened her:

The reasons I went into teaching were much more immediate last year than I think they are now.

BRAD: What were those reasons?

LIZ: Empowerment—empowering students. What good teaching meant to me as a kid, the change or the effect it had on me. What I enjoyed, the bits of school I enjoyed and my wanting to offer that to others. Social change—social change is a big, big part of that. And I don't really feel any of that now. I'm not feeling much joy about teaching. I don't get up in the morning and say, "Gosh, I love my job." I generally get up Monday and say, "Damn," or, "Okay, I get to come back [home] in x number of hours," or, "Only five more days until the weekend." It's awful, just an awful feeling. It's not what I wanted to feel about it. It's not what I wanted this to be. Last year it was something I wanted to do. This year, it's not.

As we concluded this final interview, Liz said she looked forward to summer. She hoped to sleep, reconnect with her girlfriend, sleep more, and play music. She told me she was definitely going to teach next year and made no mention of considering an exit from the profession. She simply wanted to rest and not think about classrooms for a while.

CONCLUSION

As a teacher-educator and education researcher, I find Liz's experience both troubling and understandable. Her program had more or less treated her as a blank slate—as an empty space ready to be filled with teaching ideas and approaches that would be unproblematically internalized. It neglected to acknowledge that her professional learning was in fact a complex, often emotional identity process that required excavating personal memories and role models and figuring out how to reconcile the new and often competing ideas about teaching with prior ones. Left unsupported in this endeavor, Liz was inclined to dismiss most of the newer information or to attempt to fit the familiar teaching models from her father and her own schooling into her developing professional identity. Such a move was further encouraged by the blending of personal and professional relationships. The respect she had for her father and the positive memories she had of her own English teacher, balanced against her disdain for two of the three program professors, influenced how she evaluated each person's advice.

The overriding theme from Liz's experience seems to be that beginning teachers simply have to muddle through many of the difficulties of early-career teaching. There are no easy answers for any one, nor are there any shortcuts to expertise. Quite a bit of the identity work of becoming a teacher is a kind of balancing act: working through dilemmas, reconciling prior conceptions of teaching with newer ones, adjusting the kind of teacher you have always wanted to be against the kind of teacher your students need you to be. It's a process that takes time, patience, a sense of humor, and a gritty persistence. I'm happy to report that indeed things did improve for Liz: she remained teaching at this school, benefited from joining a new teacher induction program, and after several years of teaching currently splits her time between teaching and formally mentoring new teachers at the school.

Maybe I'm overly optimistic because I've chosen this profession, but I think that good educators stay with it because it's worth the initial difficulties. Once we muddle through the first year or two and find a workable balance, sufficient joys do come to make it worthwhile. We see students grow during their year with us. We're beneficiaries of gratitude from students, parents, and school administrators. Our confidence and job satisfaction increase. The growth of professional learning and the refinement of teacher identity never end, but initial difficulties give way to new kinds of hope and new challenges. In the remaining chapters I describe other dimensions of teacher-identity development to offer support to developing teachers, so that other beginning educators are not, like Liz, left to construct their professional identities automatically and independently.

DISCUSSION QUESTIONS

1. How would you describe your own beginnings in the classroom as a teacher? What parts have been (or were) painful? What parts have been (or were) easy? What specific issues have been most pressing for you?

2. Are there any similarities between your early teaching experience and Liz's? How have you attended to them?

3. What are some of the ways in which your own personal history has helped your teacher development? What are some of the ways in which your personal history has hindered your development?

4. What are some of the strategies you have employed (or plan to employ) in order to persevere when your own teacher development gets difficult?

FURTHER READING

Grossman, P. 1990. *The Making of a Teacher: Teacher Knowledge and Teacher Education*. New York: Teachers College Press.

Johnson, S. M., and the Project on the Next Generation of Teachers. 2004. *Finders and Keepers: Helping New Teachers Survive and Thrive in Our Schools*. San Francisco: Jossey-Bass.

Lortie, D. 1975. *Schoolteacher: A Sociological Study*. Chicago: University of Chicago Press.

Michie, G. 1999. *Holler If You Hear Me: The Education of a Teacher and His Students*. New York: Teachers College Press.

CHAPTER FOUR

LEVERAGING YOUR TEACHER IDENTITY INTO A SUCCESSFUL PROFESSIONAL SELF

Teachers are making a difference. We're not only teaching these kids about content or poems or how to bake bread with their classmates or speak their minds—but how to feel good about themselves, how to make the right decisions in life. I'm so grateful to be sixty years old. I've learned lots and experienced lots. I've become a better teacher. It's a complicated world now. Children have so many pressures—from society, the planet, from their peers, and their parents. Teaching them how to be thoughtful, loving, smart people is my job. And I love my job.

—Randy, a third-grade California teacher who has been teaching for thirty-five years

PAYING ATTENTION TO the many, often hidden, aspects of your teacher identity is absolutely necessary if you're going to be successful in the complex classrooms of today. Some of that process involves learning about theory; some of it just comes from experience. In the remaining three chapters I will take a prescriptive, concrete view of teacher-identity formation. If *description* is the act of presenting and illustrating something—take it or leave it, no strings attached—then *prescription* is the act of making normative claims: telling listeners or readers what they ought to do about it. In the first half of the book I described what teacher identity can be; in the second half I will recommend how you might make it so for yourself.

In this chapter I offer a discussion on how to take ownership of your teacher identity. In Chapter 5, I will consider how you can identify and adjust your teacher identity in relation to the human, emotional dimensions of teaching as a profession. And Chapter 6 focuses on notions of race, power, culture, and critical education— how to relate your teacher identity to the current policy climate in education. As you begin this second half of the book, I hope that you'll keep the discussion in Chapter 2 about Theory and theory in mind and take the time to mindfully and explicitly work on integrating these two domains for yourself as a teacher. As you learn some *Theories* about teaching and teacher identity, try consciously putting them alongside the various *theories* that, until now, have perhaps been subtly but profoundly informing your own teacher self.

YOUR PAST MAY NOT HAVE PASSED, BUT YOUR FUTURE IS NOT YET WRITTEN

Viewing yourself through a teacher-identity lens will give you new ways to frame and improve your educational practice. An identity frame highlights views of your professional self as shaped by all sorts of personal and professional, past and present influences, yet also foregrounds a view of that self as eminently malleable—continually open to change and growth and available for improvement in the ways you desire. You are being shaped by forces, but, by understanding them, you can actively participate in the shaping of your teaching self—becoming the type of effective teacher your students need today and tomorrow.

If, as I have explained, an interpretive frame is like a pair of glasses that colors how the world looks to you, those glasses are not immutable. The pair of glasses was built over time out of innumerable life experiences and your own corresponding interpretations of them. And yet your glasses are continually being subtly adjusted, confirmed, and colored in new ways. Neglecting to notice the glasses on your head allows you to believe, erroneously, that the world that you see is actually the world that is. This makes it hard for you to see how your own experiences, personal contours, and beliefs are shaping how you approach life and how life, in turn, readjusts who you are as a person.

But once you acknowledge the existence of the glasses—once you accept that your views and ways of moving through the world are unique and that they color how many things, including teaching and learning, look to you—then you can begin to view the glasses as a constructed object. Those glasses were more or less *automatically and unconsciously* built, but they can be *intentionally and consciously* rebuilt. Applied to teaching, these glasses are your teacher identity. When you are aware of those glasses—and how they affect that ever-forming professional identity—you can analyze how your many experiences are shaping your teaching views and practices. *Your interpretive frame is suddenly made visible. This paves the way for a critical examination of that collection of influences-and-effects that this book has been calling your teacher identity—and guides you to adjust them so they're aligned with your more current, goal-oriented, Theory-informed view of yourself as an educator.*

Focus point

Of course, you are growing and changing as a teacher whether or not you actively attend to your identity.

Some of that growth simply comes from experience in the classroom and working in schools. A tenth-year teacher is naturally going to be different from a second-year teacher. She will probably diagnose students' strengths and weaknesses more quickly—and in different ways—and likely will have greater degrees of confidence and comfort. She will have developed a well-worn style in the classroom. She may also have created, honed, and saved boxes and computer files of lessons and resources. Teaching itself inevitably changes people's professional identities: often, but not always, for the better. So, too, are teachers changed by the professional development activities they experience: various workshops, good and bad; different mentors and networks of varying support and value; and books about teaching and learning all play a role. *How* a teacher interacts with and learns from that decade of teaching experience, however, is largely a function of his or her teacher identity.

The school context also carries socializing influences. Administrators, the culture of leadership at the school, students, the immediate community, recent reform activities at the school, and a teacher's relationships with colleagues all influence teacher identity. A school's material characteristics matter, too. The physical layout of a school in terms of where and how adults and children are encouraged to congregate will carry influences.

Decades of research highlight the ways in which school resources affect teachers' work. The quantity and

TEXTBOX 4.1

Picture a school with which you're familiar. How might its physical design influence the people who work there? How might a radically different architecture change the way adults and children interact—and how could those patterns of interaction in turn alter learning and teaching at the school?

age of textbooks, the equipment, and the teaching materials; the available funds for teacher salaries and professional improvement; and the upkeep of the physical spaces of a school are just some of the characteristics that separate well-funded schools from underfunded ones. These institutional factors certainly shape the work of the participating teachers.

Moreover, life itself—outside of school—plays a role in teacher development. Any teacher's ongoing personal experiences will change her over time: raising children of one's own, undergoing personal growth from skydiving or pottery classes, being influenced by friends and family, or having a side career playing jazz piano can influence one's teaching style. Sudden life changes, such as getting married, losing a loved one, or moving to a new area, will all have influences on us as people and on our teacher identities. One thing I have found as a researcher is that teachers often connect their personal hobbies (such as sports, painting, or gardening) to their teaching. This can be done well—in the case, for example, of Randy, who teaches his third graders to bake bread as a way of teaching teamwork, the value of something handmade, and good nutrition. But it can also be done badly, as in the example of a male high-school math teacher I once observed whose love for professional wrestling (and penchant for hanging graphic wrestling posters in the classroom) created a classroom culture that was uninviting to women, overly masculine, and a bit violent in tone. Such is the interrelationship between life and learning that goes into teacher-identity development.

Our experiences in life change us—that's not in question. The question is, who gets to shape the ways life changes us? How can we actively guide how our experiences will shape us as teachers? How can we assume conscious control of the teacher we're always in the process of becoming?

RECOGNIZING AND RECONSTRUCTING YOUR TEACHER IDENTITY

Identify and Examine Your Influences

Now that you know the significance of your own teacher identity, it's important that you seize some conscious control of it. You might want to catalog and examine the ongoing construction of your professional identity in much the same way that I did for Liz in Chapter 3. I realize it's often harder to examine oneself than it is to apply the analytical lens to someone else (consider how much trouble your students have when you ask them to evaluate themselves!), but it will ultimately be a rewarding and productive endeavor—again, not just for you personally and professionally but for your students, who will benefit from an improved version of you in their classroom.

First, identify what strands of personal influence have shaped, and are currently shaping, how you think about teaching and how you actually teach. I recommend using pen and paper to sketch it all out. In fact, a possible worksheet for this activity is included at the back of this book in the Appendix. Think of an *influence* as a strand of your own existence. Sometimes I call it a "life theme." It's a kind of leitmotif or force that in some way shapes you— for example, being raised in a violent household would profoundly shape a person's identity structure, or perhaps having moved from place to place a lot while growing up. It gives rise to *effects*—specific habits, perspectives, or practices that you now favor as a teacher and that appear to have fully or partially come from the influence you identified. So, for example, we could hypothesize that someone who moved around a lot as a child may have become extroverted at an early age and focused on making friends. Such an influence creates effects that then become translated into the person's teaching—he or she may have an outgoing teacher persona, or be especially friendly, or may pay extra attention to students who just moved into the community.

Another example could be how you were socialized into politics when you were younger, and the kind of political ideology you now favor; maybe you consider yourself a moderate conservative, a far-left liberal, or a libertarian. Perhaps this stance is aligned with the politics of your parents and your upbringing; perhaps it's the exact opposite. The effects of your personal politics on your teaching may include how you define "success" for yourself and also for your students, or how you conceive of teacher authority in the classroom. A political view might shape the way you respond to particular education reforms, such as English-only mandates or a standardized curriculum. It probably has an influence on how you interact with peers and parents. Your complex tangle of teacher-identity influences-and-effects is always forming and re-forming, always subtly changing yet offering a persistent guide informing your teaching and how you understand yourself professionally. In this example, teacher identity invokes your family, your upbringing, politics, and subsequent social views about educational success, learning, and teacher authority. Identify such themes and map them out. Draw lines to connect particular aspects of your personal history to current educational views you hold.

If you can identify concrete influences-and-effects like these and examine them critically—checking to see whose interests your views serve and whether each facet of your teacher identity is truly one that you want—you have made your teacher identity visible for inspection and adjustment.

To make things even more complex, the effects of the influences actually *fold back onto* the influences themselves. So an effect, in its turn, becomes another influence. This process occurs as you adjust and recalibrate the ways in which your influences (still active in the form of continually revised memories and lessons from your past) do their work. It's almost like a circle in the sense that influences create effects that then loop back to alter the power and shape of the initial influence. This is why I connect "influences-and-effects" using hyphens. I realize this is somewhat abstract (for fuller explanation, see Olsen 2010). But I'm trying to describe a kind of tangle of lines of influences-and-effects that travel through each other and keep looping back into and out of each other as they change, grow, decrease, and operate within the particular context you're in at a given moment. Imagine a loose tangle of different colored ribbons fluttering and twisting in the wind. Or reconsider the figure in Chapter 2.

By identifying your own specific strands of influence—the themes of your life, in essence—and connecting them to particular effects on, and characteristics of, your teaching and teacher self, you can examine your teacher identity and begin to reconstruct how you view those influences and the effects they have on your teacher self. This kind of teacher-identity work offers you more direct control over your professional development. It makes you more deeply mindful of the teacher you're growing into.

Family as Influence

Did you grow up around educators, such as your mom or dad, aunt or grandfather? Did your family influence you to be a teacher? Did you "play" school as a game with siblings or neighborhood children when you were young? If so, what ideas and values related to learning and teaching did you absorb, and what did being an educator mean to those who surrounded you when you were young? Even though that was a long time ago and in a very different context, vestiges of those experiences may still remain. I suspect that your family's beliefs and practices around education have entered into who you are now in various ways. How did you feel about those educational beliefs and values then? How do you feel about them now? Have you felt conflict between your family's ideas about teaching and learning and your own current views, or between the views of instructors in your teacher-education program and your colleagues in school?

Can you identify particular aspects of your current teaching that come from views of teaching influenced by your family or upbringing? Are you proud of those influences—happy to have them actively influencing you? Or might they be problematic? If your family members who were educators are still around, sit down and talk with them about the ideas in this book. I would bet that everyone will learn powerful things both about themselves and about education simply through that dialogue. Even if your family members aren't educators, their general values, perspectives, and ways of raising you surely produced lasting conceptions of the world that influence your teaching now. Maybe your family instilled notions of fairness or diversity or hard work that have become (mostly unexamined) cornerstones of your own teaching philosophy.

In my research I've found that many teachers experience acute teacher-identity conflicts in their first and second years of teaching. And I've found that these conflicts—misgivings and negotiations about what kind of teacher one wants to be, can be, or is becoming—result from having to automatically reconcile long-held conceptions of teaching and learning with one's new, current teaching reality. One first-year high-school English teacher named Tara found that the process of making this switch was exciting, but hard. She had to replace deeply held, traditional views of teaching with newer and better (but less familiar) ones: "I used to 'play' teacher when I was a kid. I remember giving fake quizzes a lot. It wasn't about discussion; it was about making fake report cards and having the power and bossing the other kids around. Now, that stuff—quizzes, grading, et cetera—is what I like the least about teaching. There's been tension as I started to realize that teaching isn't what I thought it was. Not disappointment, just surprise and wonder."

These conflicts can be emotionally taxing. And what's
worse is that educators rarely discuss them, and teacher-
preparation programs typically don't raise them officially—
or even let their novices know that such identity conflicts
will arise. Too often teachers are left to recognize, work
through, and manage these professional-identity dilemmas
by themselves. It doesn't have to be this way; everyone in
education should find ways to openly acknowledge and
talk through the many dimensions of these early-career
teacher-identity conflicts. I hope that you will find ways to
talk with your colleagues about conflicts between your
long-held views of teaching and your current classroom

Focus point

situation. *If you engage in these types of discussions, then you
will quickly find that you are not alone in dealing with the
challenges and anxieties of reconciling an ongoing set of conflicting viewpoints. You might even develop a greater sense of
peace knowing that working through these conflicts is actually
something that is embedded in the process of becoming a better
teacher.*

Didactic Teaching versus Constructivist Teaching

One of the major struggles for teachers occurs in the internal and ongoing tension between didactic teaching
and constructivist teaching. This was in large part what
happened for Liz, as discussed in Chapter 3—and, for
her (as for many others), it mapped onto a tension between prior, family-related teaching models and contemporary, research-based models.

The history of education in our country is steeped in a
didactic, transfer model of teaching and learning where the
dominant pedagogy has too often been about passing on
some autonomous body of knowledge to be received and
warehoused in passive students, as if knowledge were like
cans of beans in an empty stockroom. Yet, ever since educators such as John Dewey, Maria Montessori, and
Paulo Freire arrived on the scene, there has been an alternative paradigm: teaching as providing crafted opportu-

nities for students to interrogate the world for themselves
and construct their own resultant understandings of and
orientations to it. It is inside this alternate history—
sometimes termed *constructivism* or *critical pedagogy*—
that many progressive educators focus their teaching.

Though there are certainly exceptions, I have found
that this tension between the two teaching paradigms often emerges in ways similar to what happened for Liz.
Many of the teachers I've studied were themselves educated inside the didactic, "traditional" model of teaching
where knowledge was treated as an entity that could be
transferred from expert teachers (and textbooks) to
blank-slate students. From this it follows that a teacher
should lecture, assign quizzes and simple activities, and
push students in drills to practice their new learning—
while students should listen, internalize the knowledge,
and follow preset instructions. This model also tends to
accept that successful teaching necessitates controlling
the class and demanding obedience under notions of "respect" for the material, for schooling, or for the institutional authority of the teacher.

But many educationalists and educators reject this
"deliver the content and control the kids" paradigm of
teaching and replace it with a more constructivist one.
Progressive, constructivist teachers and teacher-educators
support a view of learners as inherently curious, active
knowledge-builders who succeed by engaging authentically, even clumsily at times, yet always meaningfully,
with real questions and activities about the world. These
educators believe that true learning is noisy, social, frequently messy, and rarely linear. They believe that teachers who dominate students will limit students' ability to
actively engage with the material or to become comfortable enough to take risks, try new ideas, and speak up for
themselves.

As Paulo Freire (1970) wrote, "Authentic education is
not carried on by [the teacher] *for* [students] or by [the
teacher] *about* [students], but rather by [the teacher]

with [students], mediated by the world—a view which impresses and challenges both parties, giving rise to views or opinions about it" (93). In other words, the teacher must act as a student and encourage the students to be teachers, as much as the other way around. Only when there is authentic dialogue between students and teacher as real people engaged in authentic activity about the real world around them, argued Freire, is there true learning.

For Liz, it was this divide between traditional and constructivist models of teaching that framed a large part of her struggle over how to make sense of her dad's teaching approach against the one her teacher-education program espoused. I've found that other teachers face a similar conflict today. Many teachers experienced traditional, didactic settings as children, and yet their teacher-education programs, and—if they're lucky—the schools that now employ them, operate within a more progressive, constructivist teaching paradigm. Making the transition is difficult, and a kind of identity crisis often occurs as part of the process of working it out.

Check to see if some version of this common pedagogical conflict is in play for you. If so, using ideas and techniques from this book, try to excavate the deeper origins of this conflict to see how it's affecting your teacher identity. You may have to work hard to adjust, reconstruct, or eliminate those silent, yet strongly held views of learning and teaching that do not match up with the teacher you want to be.

Even if you did not grow up around educators, there are still many personal influences from family and the communities in which you were raised that have surely shaped how you think about education now. Find and catalog those influences. If you do not take the time to understand them, they may silently control you as a teacher, shaping your daily planning, instruction, and interactions in the school without your knowledge. As a result, you might end up habitually creating the "perfect lesson" for yourself, as if *you* were the learner—but as we well know, you're not teaching a classroom full of your clones. By contrast, if you do take the time to understand the various influences that form your teacher identity, you will be better able to adjust the planning process to reduce your natural teaching tendencies and thus will be able to consider and address the learning needs of a broader range of students.

Teaching the American Dream: Myth or Reality?

Like many middle-class, twentieth-century children in the United States, I was raised to believe in some version of the American Dream. In the American Dream, success was initially about what the Founding Fathers termed "life, liberty, and the pursuit of happiness"—and success in America still retains parts of that: living an honorable life in the United States and working hard are expected to bring a person material comforts and psychic rewards. Overall, this strong cultural influence (and resulting belief system) might strike the casual observer as positive and uplifting, at best, or innocent and innocuous, at worst. Yet it's exactly this type of unexamined influence that can significantly impact one's teacher identity and classroom instruction. In fact, such a belief can impact teacher identity more profoundly than we might ever imagine. I would like to share some details from my own personal pilgrimage in developing a teacher identity to illustrate how even the simple notion of the American Dream can shape us as teachers in almost unconscious ways.

When I was young, I was taught that future success and happiness were within my grasp as long as I worked hard, played by the rules, and respected the social structures of society. If I did my part, I would be rewarded. The society in which I lived subtly suggested to me that unsuccessful people—those on the margins, homeless on the street, out of work, or otherwise having a hard time of things—were in these dismal situations by their own volition. They didn't work hard, or didn't respect the structures of society, or somehow didn't make good use of their talents. Such a belief system works well for those whose values, worldviews, cultures, and personal characteristics correspond to the culture of power: Anglos and other white Americans, men, heterosexuals, members of the middle or upper-middle class. Such people did indeed often find that the culture of power matched their values, beliefs, and views of the world. And so they achieved a kind of success that they could readily attribute to their own "hard work and honest living"—even if, in fact, it wasn't quite that simple.

When I was a child, such a view more or less made sense to me. It was never critiqued or deconstructed for me, and my own social class, gender, and cultural milieu meant that I stood to be on the receiving end of the belief system's benefits. My great-grandparents had immigrated from Norway with little to their name. They had done okay materially and otherwise by playing by the rules and were able to provide for their children. Although my parents are ethical, progressive, and honorable people, there was not a lot in my personal history to cause me to critically interrogate the American Dream and its link to notions of personal and material success. However, beginning in the 1980s, many cultural critics emerged who argued that the American Dream had become synonymous with consumerism, self-interest, and a set of social indicators commensurate with historical domination at the hands of what the author and feminist bell hooks (1981) has called a "white-supremacist-capitalist-patriarchy." And I soon became exposed to new people and different views in my life as well as various books and experiences that encouraged me to reexamine what the American Dream meant and whose interests it served.

As a result, I now see the American Dream in far more ambivalent terms—probably somewhere in the middle of the two extremes I just described. It still resonates in some ways as the hopes and possibilities for a democratic ideal inherent in the promise of the United States. But it also stands as a hegemonic myth or ideology that keeps the masses in line: that dangles material success and eternal happiness in front of people like carrots in order to discourage them from revolting or opting out of dominant, often oppressive norms, values, and social practices in this country.

How did this looming tower of my own personal history affect my teacher identity? Well, that's an easy question for me to answer. I was raised at home and in school to believe that my success or failure in life hinged primarily on me. Academic achievement (or its absence) depended primarily on individual initiative, not on the ways in which schools were organized or on cultural factors. In other words, I was encouraged to believe that success was not about the degree to which my belief system corresponded to that of the dominant culture; it was, instead, about me—how well (or badly) I did in school, how hard (or not) I worked to become the person I was expected to be. IQ tests purported to measure my smarts. I "earned" various grades and scores that located me on hierarchical stepladders of the GPAs, SATs, and even the ASVAB.

My parents, teachers, and the society around me told me to study harder, not cheat, believe in myself, and accept no limits on what I was capable of achieving. I was socialized to believe that the system in place in this country—the laws, norms, schools and other institutions, and various social structures—treated everyone

TEXTBOX 4.2

GPA is grade point average. SAT originally stood for Scholastic Aptitude Test; the test has since been renamed and is currently called the SAT Reasoning Test. ASVAB is the Armed Services Vocational Aptitude Battery.

equally and according to merit. If I respected the system, it would respect me. If I supported it, it would support me.

I was therefore predisposed as a young teacher to view social success and failure, academic achievement and mediocrity, in these same terms for my students. Students were more or less autonomous individuals who rose or fell in the classroom based on their own individual wills. If they were not succeeding, it was their fault, and my job as a teacher was to do my best to motivate them, and then to evaluate them. The same was true for classroom behavior. If their actions didn't correspond to the norms and rules of the school, I was supposed to straighten them out. It was their fault (or perhaps the fault of their parents or other caregivers who could then be disparaged for "not raising those kids right"). If their actions did correspond to what the school and, by extension, the society desired, then these hardworking (and obedient) students were to be congratulated and promoted along. These ideas about success in school were also more or less what my graduate teacher-education program emphasized, which means that my program acted to confirm the legitimacy of this bundle of beliefs about education that I carried with me into the profession.

A year or two into my teaching, however, I developed a different view of how discrimination and liberation operate within the educational practices of the United States. These critical, more sociopolitical views, which resulted from conversations I'd had with others, reflections on my own teaching, and a series of critical readings (such as Samuel Bowles and Herbert Gintis's *Schooling in Capitalist America* [1975], Jonathan Kozol's *Savage Inequalities* [1991], and Paul Willis's *Learning to Labour* [1981]), caused me to reconsider both the American Dream and my own teacher identity—and ultimately helped me to create a deeper, more effective set of teaching practices. As a teacher I began recognizing that students are, in their own ways, responding to larger family, cultural, and political influences as they are developing their selves in and out of the classroom. I talked with students about how social history shapes which knowledge is validated and which is marginalized in schools. I encouraged students to think about working for their own educational successes instead of conforming merely to get good grades or other kinds of positive, extrinsic reinforcement. I opened up the curriculum and put more responsibility for classroom success on the students themselves.

I don't wish to belabor this perhaps obvious example. And I'm not suggesting that this happens to all new teachers—or that I am some kind of super-teacher (which I am not). And of course it's not as simple as this gloss suggests. But I want to say that it took time to begin to understand these social influences and their impact on my teacher identity. With time, several provocative books and experiences, and rigorous self-examination, I was able to reconstruct this aspect of my professional identity into a different view of how culture, race, economics, and sociohistory operate in schools. I began to embrace a more student-centered, critical model that shares the power with students and includes examination of the ways that dominant groups perpetuate their power. I still have work to do on the journey. Like all teachers, I'm still becoming.

There are countless examples like this one in my own teacher development where now I recognize that I was still learning how to interpret and navigate the complex social and learning worlds of my classrooms: how to interpret gender dominance in my classroom, how to react to authority conflicts in the classroom, how to understand students who seem disengaged or resistant, how to simultaneously support and challenge students. All students—mine and yours—deserve a teacher who has made his or her influences and effects the objects of sustained, critical examination.

Your Own Schooling as Influence

Family and early socialization experiences have surely
been intertwined with your own *K–12 school and college
experiences* such that all of them now overlap and confirm
each other, or, perhaps, clash and create conflict for you
as an early-career teacher. *I recommend that you conduct a*

Focus point *critical inventory of the kinds of beliefs, values, and understandings about teaching and learning that you absorbed
from your own schooling and that you may now rely on in
subtle but profound ways.* As we saw in Chapter 3, Liz's
views of teaching and learning were strongly shaped by
her own schooling experiences. I presume that you have
already spent considerable time reflecting on the kind of
learner you were in elementary and high school and pon-
dered how that currently shapes your teaching. Try engaging in this kind of reflection again, this time through
the lens of this book, and push yourself to be critical and
probing of the vestigial lessons you're still carrying
around with you. It may be that your default teacher
identity privileges students who learn the same way you
did—and inadvertently penalizes or neglects those with
learning styles different from yours. The same is surely
true—as I will take up in Chapter 6—for issues of ethnicity, race, culture, sexuality, and gender.

Your time at the university also contributed, both directly and indirectly, to your current understandings of
teaching and learning. Below we look at the example of a
beginning teacher named Azar, a young Iranian woman
raised in California. Her story shows how one's high-
school and college experiences can combine to strongly
inform the kind of teacher one becomes.

Azar's Schooling

In high school, Azar found acceptance through academic
success. The small, private school she attended was a
close community that valued the kind of serious academ-

ics with which she was already comfortable: "Part of [why I felt included there] was because academics was very much a part of the culture. There wasn't a sense of, like, segregation because you like to read, or because you did well." Azar valued the teachers there who "related to us as people," "formed a personal connection with a lot of students," or "related to students on more than just a teacher-student relationship." She began to equate effective teaching with forming candid, personal bonds with students and caring about them deeply. She also located her own sociable nature in her family: "It's very personable in my family. Friends come over and my family's like, 'Stay for dinner!' I think that's why it's so easy for me to connect to students in the classroom."

During her time at the university, Azar underwent an awakening that radicalized her politically. She already had a personal interest in the power of community, but this interest was now transformed into an educational philosophy. Specifically, there were six sources of influence on her teacher identity that came from her college experience: her education minor, her psychology major, her tutoring work, her community outreach participation, her martial arts classes, and the university's political climate. These college influences, both separately and together, helped to develop her views of community and her desire to, in her words, "create a revolution" through teaching. Of particular influence was the community outreach work she did during college. Going into local group homes and talking with teenagers caused her to begin to link *communities* as her learning frame with *political empowerment* as her primary goal as a teacher. It also convinced her that many marginalized teenagers face systematic discrimination. This is the mindset she brought with her into her graduate teacher-education program, which she entered not six weeks after finishing college.

There isn't the space here to go into great detail about Azar's schooling experiences or exactly how they influenced the kind of beginning teacher that Azar became. But her

example might offer a quick lesson into how to look for—
and examine—high-school and college experiences that
may be actively yet quietly shaping your current view of
yourself as a teacher.

Kim's Tutoring

Another powerful influence on many early-career teachers
is time they have spent working with children in informal
learning contexts. Tutoring kids, working as a summer
camp counselor, being an athletic coach, and working
with young people in other recreational or educational
settings can serve as an introduction to what it means to
be a role model, how learning works, and the like. These
experiences are valuable—tutoring and counseling jobs
recruit young adults into the teaching profession; they offer children powerful mentorship opportunities; they can
introduce future teachers to what it means to form personal relationships with students or to see kids succeed
outside the classroom. Yet, uninterrogated, they can also
allow in certain conceptions of teaching and learning that
can lead to teacher-identity conflicts in the classroom
later on. A first-year middle-school teacher named Kim, a
Chinese American from California, found this to be true
for her.

Upon graduating from a university, Kim had taken a
job working in an after-school tutoring program for middle-school students. She wasn't necessarily planning to
become a teacher, but she needed a job and found the job
posting online. As it turned out, she loved her work as a
tutor, and as a result she decided to become a middle-
school language arts teacher. The job also set in motion
some views of education that went on to cause Kim difficulty as a first-year teacher:

> As a tutor I had thirty students for about three hours
> every afternoon . . . kids in sixth and seventh grade deal-
> ing with gangs and a lot of those issues that go on in

junior high and middle school but that adults dismiss as petty, [so] I decided to change the after-school program into more of a social-justice program. We researched our community in terms of stereotypes about race and gangs. It went very well, and after that whole experience, I felt like I wanted to do this forever.

Embedded in this experience was an identity transformation that shaped Kim's teaching views. During her teacher-education year, she defined herself as "a social-justice teacher" and said this was because of her prior work in the after-school program, and she described herself as an anti-teacher teacher: "During the after-school program I developed a bad impression of teachers because, [listening to students, I learned that] a lot of the teachers they had were not the type of teacher I wanted to be. So when I [decided to] be a teacher, I had this idea of being the cool one, being more on their side than the teachers' side."

These particular views of teaching, however—being friends with students; raising topics like race, bias, and hegemony; striving to be the "cool one" at the expense of "typical" teachers—became problematic during Kim's first year of teaching, when she was working in a relatively traditional, academically focused public school:

Now I'm finding that it's really hard to draw that line where, even though students and I have a lot in common, like [a love of] video games, it doesn't mean that we're automatically going to be friends, even if we get along well outside the classroom: In the classroom I'm still their teacher, still an authority figure. Just because they're goofing off and I think it's funny doesn't mean they're going to get away with it. For me it's been really difficult this year and really difficult for students to realize that I'm the teacher and not their friend. It's hard for me to set them straight sometimes because my [tutoring] background allowed me to be a friend, and I think I like that relationship better, but as a teacher I can't do that.

Kim's incoming emphases on informal learning and social justice education led to some conflicts for her as a teacher. One was that she had difficulty reconciling her internal tendency to be a fun friend to students with her professional role as the authority figure in the classroom. A second conflict was that Kim believed her social justice commitments were incompatible with her school district's emphasis on high test scores. The mandated focus on academic standards and test scores left almost no room in the curriculum, Kim believed, for her social justice interests. The last time we spoke, Kim told me she felt frustrated working at this school and did not know how long she would remain there.

Current Personal Experiences

The important work of developing your teacher identity should also lead you to examine your social relationships with others and your current personal experiences.

TEXTBOX 4.3

Who do you "talk teaching" with? What do you talk about? Are there particular patterns that can be identified in your own comments about your teaching when you are talking with others? Do you find yourself circling back to the same topics, the same issues or debates, over and over again? If so, what could that mean? What are the underlying perspectives about education that *sit below* your comments and those of your conversationalists? Serious consideration of these questions will allow you to begin to notice your teacher identity. Dig for the *deeper conceptions* of teaching and learning held by you and by educators who surround you. Look for conflicts—places where you disagree, or where others' perspectives don't quite sit right with you. Might these disagreements or misalignments illuminate something significant going on? Maybe differing assumptions about education or different professional identities?

Spend time thinking about your teacher identity against the educational philosophies and teaching practices of your colleagues and friends.

How about other aspects of your life? What do you do for fun? How do your relationships with family and friends affect who you're becoming in the classroom? Those things you do that at first glance may seem to have little to do with you as a professional educator are undoubtedly influencing your teacher self. In some cases, you're drawing from these personal activities and relationships for lesson ideas—activities, questions, and examples for use in the classroom. I can't tell you how many activity ideas and writing prompts I have received from eavesdropping on conversations in buses and subways or from reading newspapers or signs on the street. If you're looking for them, teaching ideas are everywhere! Some ideas for educational activities that I picked up from childhood games and popular culture are mentioned in Textbox 4.4.

Your moods, the things you think about, and the kind of life you're leading can all find their way into the classroom in productive ways for your students. The general point is that the more conscious and reflective you can be about the life experiences happening around you and the ways in which the various aspects of who you are as a person enter into your teacher identity, the more intentional and thoughtful a teacher you will become. And the fact is, as you will see below, your personal life does influence who you are in the classroom.

Elena's Neighbor

I knew a fifth-grade teacher in her sixth year of teaching in California who found herself being ornery and impatient with her students. Her name was Elena, and she wondered what was happening; this was not the kind of teacher she had always been in the past. Eventually, I asked her about her personal life. It turned out that a dear friend, her close

---

TEXTBOX 4.4   ACTIVITY IDEAS

LEARNING REVIEW BASEBALL. Go outside and play "baseball" with real bases but no bats or balls. Divide students into two or more teams. You're the pitcher. Each batter can choose the degree of difficulty of the pitch (a single, double, triple, or home-run attempt) and you "pitch" by asking the batter a question of corresponding difficulty. A right answer sends the player to the requisite base; a wrong answer is an out. Three outs and the next team is up. Teams alternate taking turns at bat until the game ends. I used to play this game with students to review for the final exam on Shakespeare.

LEARNING REVIEW DUCK DUCK GOOSE. Go outside, sit in a circle, and play duck duck goose, but with a twist: the student who taps another person on the head also asks a learning-related question and then slowly circles the group. If the person tapped fails to answer the question before the questioner completes the circle, then the tapped student becomes "it." I used this game to review units on Greek mythology, poetry, and writing rules.

JEOPARDY. Develop your own game and set up teams.

SCAVENGER HUNTS. Have students search for items around the school with academic questions as clues.

---

neighbor who lived in the apartment below, was in the hospital dying from a protracted illness. Elena was sad and a little angry at having to see such a good person leave the world early. As we talked more, she recognized that this experience was leaving her with a kind of resentment toward life: the world isn't fair—why do the good people have to leave us early? And without consciously realizing it, her mood had overtaken her teaching self and was coloring her interactions with students.

Although I'm no therapist (and would never claim to be one), I did want her to remember all the positive aspects of her friendship with her neighbor, so I asked questions to learn about this neighbor's life. It turns out that dozens of people had known and cared about and been cared for by this person over the years. According to Elena, everyone who knew this woman was better off because of it. A new way of including this friend into Elena's teacher identity was revealing itself! We talked about what the children might have learned had they spent time with her friend.

Before long, Elena was thinking about how to honor her neighbor and include this neighbor's life-affirming example in her own teaching. Elena talked to her students about her friend, hung a photo of the friend in the classroom, and modeled some of her friend's characteristics in the classroom: Elena wrote "Carpe Diem!" on the classroom wall and encouraged her students to take on new challenges daily and to always be good to others. She hung posters of German expressionist paintings in the room because that's the art her friend loved. Though it took some time, as well as some soul-searching, Elena had found a way to use her own personal experience to continue to work toward becoming the teacher she wanted to be. And I'm certain that these children benefited from Elena's ability to reconstruct how her experience was shaping her teacher identity. I know that I did, and I still think of Elena's neighbor every time I see a picture of Gustav Klimt's painting *The Kiss*, even though I never met her myself.

ORGANIZING, EXAMINING, AND TALKING ABOUT THE INTERRELATED PARTS OF TEACHER IDENTITY

Using the notes you've taken thus far on the sources of your teacher identity, you can now begin to organize and reassemble your understanding of your own identity development. Again, think about it in terms of *influences and effects*. What strands of your past and present, personal and professional experience are subtly but perhaps profoundly shaping how you think teaching and learning are "supposed to" happen? How are your various influences interacting with (perhaps confirming or maybe conflicting with) each other? Use the worksheet included at the end of this book. Perhaps draw and fill out your own version of Figure 2.1.

One goal is to consciously consider which influences benefit you as a teacher and which ones work against you. Each of us carries remnants from our youth that are incompatible with who we are now and who we want to become. These remnants generally take the form of old ideas and views that we haven't yet gotten around to fully shedding—even though, when we view them soberly in the light of day, we don't believe them. In terms of cognition, Howard Gardner (1991) calls these "naïve learner theories." (Consider novelist Wallace Stegner's thoughtful line: "A prejudice is a principle its owner does not intend to examine" [1990, 156].) It's hard to acknowledge these parts of ourselves. And it's all too easy to ignore these tendencies that so many of us still possess, because the society we live in has done a number on us: it's convinced us that certain ways of being are "normal" or "natural" while others are "deviant," "wrong," or "inappropriate."

Vestiges from our personal history carry embedded views of concrete aspects of teaching and learning, too: what a "successful" classroom looks and sounds like, how to decorate our classrooms, how to teach a unit on Asia or the recent economic collapse, how we assess students, why and how to tell students to "be quiet," what homework to assign.

DIRECT AND MEDIATING EFFECTS OF INFLUENCES

As you explore these issues you should recognize and address both the direct and indirect influences on your teacher identity. A *direct influence* is an influence that derives from some part of your personal or professional history, your schooling, or your teacher preparation that contains a specific understanding or perspective on teaching that you have accepted or adopted as part of your identity. An education professor who taught you to put a learning agenda on the board for students each day—and also explained some of the theory behind such an action—is offering you a bundle of information that you might take and begin using. It's more straightforward than an indirect influence. These direct influences are easiest to notice, monitor, evaluate, keep, modify, or reject.

But influences on teacher identity can be mediating, too. *Indirect influences* are harder to tease out because they become interwoven with others. Knowing where one influence ends and the other begins, as you reflect on your professional self, is not easy. Indirect influences are less visible and less certain than direct influences. But this may be where the real work is required. For example, an education professor might teach you about Jean Piaget's theory of cognitive development in children. You may be taught something about accommodation versus assimilation; you might have looked at some of Piaget's observations of children playing with objects; you may have listened to your professor talk about how children develop abstractions by performing tasks over and over again with increasing complexity. But how you actually make sense of Piaget's theory of learning also invokes your own preexisting ideas about learning—coming from sources such as your own experiences as a child, the ways your teachers taught you, and even some of your feelings about the particular professor who is teaching Piaget to you. Your learning of Piaget's theories does not involve direct internalization of educational theory but is rather a mediated, multifaceted construction of your interpretation of Piaget's ideas in relation to your own ideas about and experiences in the world. To notice and thoroughly examine these indirect influences—and how they affect the different parts of your teacher identity—requires patience, but it's worth the effort.

CONCLUSION

There is only so much that we can learn about ourselves by ourselves. It's important to engage others, too, in collective reflection about your teacher identity. Your job requires that you become a reflective practitioner, someone who engages in collective reflection and collaborative practice. Identify peers in your teacher-education program or colleagues at your school whom you trust who might be willing to engage in conversations about teacher identity. Ask them to join you in a dialogue about teacher development. Each person involved in this dialogue should be willing to explore his or her own teacher identity and to help others do the same. Create teacher-identity inquiry groups in your school, or encourage your professors and network facilitators to engage already-existing groups (such as classes or cohort meetings) in coordinated teacher-identity reflection.

Whatever the setting, find ways to initiate substantive conversations around questions such as those included below, and take notes on the results so that you can return to the insights later, on your own, to deeply consider how to acknowledge, evaluate, and adjust the ways in which your personal history shapes your teacher perspectives.

DISCUSSION QUESTIONS

1. What are my personal influences offering me in terms of specific models of teaching on which I might be relying? Which influences-and-effects should I retain? Which should I jettison?

2. What are five facets of my own teaching philosophy, and where do those beliefs come from?

3. How do my personal politics enter into my teaching? Do they limit or enhance the learning of my students?

4. How do my own past experiences in schools shape the way I think about my students? Do they limit or enhance the learning of my students?

5. Which of my current, now-visible teacher-identity features do I want to retain? Which do I want to eliminate? And which do I want to adjust?

6. How, specifically, will I make the changes I need to make? And what evidence will I look for to evaluate the success of those changes?

7. How will I be sure to continue this kind of teacher reflection and identity adjustment in the future? Can I find others to do it with me?

FURTHER READING

Ayers, B. 2001. *To Teach: The Journey of a Teacher*. New York: Teachers College Press.

Brookfield, S. 2006. *The Skillful Teacher*. San Francisco: Jossey-Bass.

Huberman, M. 1993. *The Lives of Teachers*. Translated by J. Neufeld. New York: Teachers College Press.

Lipka, R., and T. Brinthaupt, eds. 1999. *The Role of Self in Teacher Development*. Albany: State University of New York Press.

CHAPTER FIVE

THE HUMAN DIMENSIONS OF TEACHING AND IDENTITY

I believe we teach who we are. And so as a teacher you must find ways to be who you are in ways that benefit your students.
—Randy, a third-grade California teacher who has been teaching for thirty-five years

WHAT KIND OF TEACHER ARE YOU, OR HOW DO YOU GO ABOUT FINDING OUT?

It has come up again and again in this book: who you are as a person has a lot to do with who you are as a teacher. From this truism come many themes that are important to your teacher development. One theme is the need to recognize the fact that *your personal self is a significant source of your professional self.* This is probably both good and bad, and making successful use of this fact hinges on your ability to purposefully manage how you allow aspects of your personal self and your personal history to enter into your professional self. This theme has been the central concern of this book because, without that understanding,

I recommend that you actively manage the ways in which your teaching work seeps into your personal life.

you will find it difficult to maximize your potential impact on student learning.

A second theme revolves around the fact that *your professional life will inevitably affect your personal life* (and vice versa). Teachers report that their good days at school often lead to improved moods in the evenings and on weekends. Conversely, those bad days at work—and all of us teachers have them, lots of them in fact, as they're a natural part of the job description—can leave you in a foul mood after the school day ends. In Chapter 3 we learned that Liz's difficulties as a first-year teacher placed a strain on her personal life. In Chapter 4, I wrote about Elena's personal sadness creeping into her classroom interactions with children. I recommend that you actively manage the ways in which your teaching work seeps into your personal life. Randy, the third-grade teacher whose quote appeared at the beginning of this chapter, told me that "teaching is exhausting. You get exhausted by the end of the day. You need to talk with your significant other and explain that there are particular things that you need when you get home. For me, it's a pot of tea ready for me and a quiet corner for thirty minutes. I don't want to be asked how my day was; I don't want to talk about anything; I just want half an hour to relax by myself and then I can rejoin the world."

Successful teachers also find ways to ensure that negative events in their personal lives don't carry over into the classroom in ways that make them ornery or less patient with students. I remember a difficult day of my own in the 1990s, when during lunch I received a letter with sad news (I was teaching abroad and using the school as my mailing address). Having about ten minutes to process the information and compose myself before my fifth-period class began, I found an unused office and sat by myself for a few minutes, working to separate my suddenly terrible mood from the two dozen wonderful students I was about to greet; I knew that they didn't deserve to have me dampen their learning that day just because I was depressed. I convinced myself that I could put aside my negative feelings until the end of the day and focus instead on the students in front of me. Not only was it the right thing to do as a teacher, but it also lifted my spirits a bit so that later, when I returned to the sad news, I felt somewhat better. In addition, this event and my reflection upon it reminded me that I must see my students as whole people too. Just as teachers lead complex lives that can affect their work, so too are students grappling daily with the slings and arrows of their own lives both inside and outside of school. It's important for me not to forget that.

A third theme that follows from the truism about teaching and personhood being inextricably linked is the core fact that, in many ways, the successful teaching-learning relationship is a strongly personal endeavor on both sides—the teaching part and the learning part. For all the professional training, specialized knowledge, research implications, and policy demands of education work, teaching and learning are at their heart largely human processes. And this means that education is about human relationships as much as it is about evidence-based curricula, learning-sensitive assessment, and educational reform policies. Throughout the history of teaching, there have been hundreds of books and articles emphasizing the ways in which teaching can be informed by love, passion, and other fundamentally humanist dimensions (see, for example, Palmer 1998; Freire 1970; and hooks 1994). This isn't, of course, to say that teaching is not a specialized profession requiring technical knowledge and focused training; it is. But alongside the specialized, technical dimensions of teaching is the need to enact one's humanness in ways that create a rich, rigorous, comfortable learning environment that supports children in their own growth.

Almost 150 years ago, Horace Mann (1868) wrote that "a teacher who is attempting to teach without inspiring the pupil with a desire to learn is hammering on a cold

The successful teaching-learning relationship is a strongly personal endeavor on both sides—the teaching part and the learning part.

iron." Maybe the authoritarian imagery of this black-
smith metaphor is a little rough (I'd hate to consider students as metal to be pounded), but we might interpret it
to mean that the job of teaching is largely about inspiring
learning, which requires honest, respectful, reciprocal human relationships between teacher and students.

In an interview with Bill Moyers, educator and author
Mike Rose talked about teaching as a kind of romance,
not toward another person per se but in terms of fostering loving relationships with knowledge and curiosity:

> MOYERS: You write that teaching is a romance.
> ROSE: Yes it *is* a romance. It's a romance, the terms of
> which are language, mathematical formulas, facts, dates,
> theories, opinions. It's easy to lose faith in that. . . . The
> way I view education is as an invitation. It is an attempt
> to bring people into a kind of conversation, into a set of
> ideas, into ways of thinking, talking, writing and reading
> that are new to them. If you see education as an attempt
> to bring people in, then you automatically see it as a re-
> lationship. And if the relationship works right, it is a
> kind of romance. (Moyers 1990, 218)

Similarly, many of educator Paulo Freire's writings focus
on his belief that true love for humanity is a necessary
precondition for enacting education as liberation. A
teacher becomes an authentic educator for liberation
only once he has recognized in himself a true love for all
people—and especially those he is teaching. And, finally,
building off Freire and making an explicit link to teach-
ings from Buddhist monk Thich Nhat Hanh, educator
and author bell hooks argued that an effective teacher is
in part a "healer" helping students to integrate mind,
body, and spirit amid a splintered, hurtful world. But not
only must teachers help their students, they must help
themselves too. In hooks's words: "Teachers must be actively committed to a process of self-actualization that
promotes their own well-being if they are to teach in a

manner that [heals and] empowers students. Thich Nhat Hanh emphasized that 'the practice of a healer, therapist, teacher or any helping professional should be directed toward his or her self first, because if the helper is unhappy, he or she cannot help many people'" (hooks 1994, 15).

In this chapter I use the teacher-identity model to highlight significant ways in which teachers can acknowledge and make productive use of their "humanness" in their professional work. By "humanness" I mean to invoke those many aspects of our personal selves, including our relational selves and the emotional sides of us, that enter into our teaching. Of course, everything that humans do is, by definition, "human." However, I use the term here to foreground those aspects of successful teaching that don't always appear in the research literature or in textbooks about formal education processes, but which any practicing teacher knows are always in play, actively shaping the work of teaching and learning. It's our responsibility to ensure that our personal characteristics don't act as negative influences but rather become productive, empathetic parts of our work.

I begin by considering the legacy of Carl Rogers and *humanistic psychology* for teaching: the humanistic perspective offers a caring way to emphasize the "whole person" in teaching and to stress the human qualities of

---

TEXTBOX 5.1

Few occupations rest as centrally on personal relationships for their professional success as teaching. But there are others. Researchers and educators have written about similarities between teaching and preaching, or about teaching's connections to therapy, midwifery, being a football quarterback, and medicine (Belenky et al. 1986; Coles and Testa 2002; Gladwell 2008; Grossman et al. 2009; Noddings 2003). Can you think of other professions whose core work centrally hinges on its personal relationships?

learning. Next I discuss *emotions in teaching and teacher burnout* so that you can think about how your own emotions and those of your students affect your teaching and your career. And, third, I review the psychological concept of *self-efficacy* in order to assist you in recognizing your teaching confidence—because, after all, the kind of teacher you *expect to be* shapes the teacher you'll actually become. Expecting the best from yourself encourages you to become the best you can be.

I recommend that as you read this chapter and the one that follows—which focuses on the political and cultural aspects of your teacher identity—you attempt to place yourself inside the discussions. Have these things happened to you? How adept are you at noticing how your human qualities interact with your professional self? What will you do to integrate both sides in ways that serve students successfully, and to do this more often and more deeply?

HUMANISTIC PSYCHOLOGY AND TEACHING

Humanistic psychology emerged in the late 1950s as a branch of psychology focusing on sensitivity to the whole person. Unlike psychotherapy and behaviorism, which were popular strands of American psychology at the time, humanistic psychology focused on the holistic self-actualization and creativity of an individual. Whereas traditional psychology was mostly concerned with what limits people, humanistic psychology emphasized self-empowerment, creativity, and nonconformity. Carl Rogers is considered the founder of this branch of psychology and did the most to outline humanistic psychology and explicitly identify the conditions under which humans can achieve their full potential (see, for example, *The Freedom to Learn*, 1969). Though its influence on teaching and human development has waned over the decades or was swallowed up into other movements (such as Gestalt psychology or positive psychology), it continues to offer teachers some powerful ideas.

Humanistic psychology views individuals as inherently good. People are innately cooperative, trustworthy, empathetic, and interested in improving themselves. But Rogers and his contemporaries believed that these tendencies need to be actively released—they're not just activated by themselves. The immediate environment must encourage trust, self-confidence, and comfort. If these conditions are met, a person can work toward becoming what Rogers termed a "fully functioning person." To be fully functioning, a person would be open to experience and always looking for the newness and possibility of each moment. She would be confident enough to take chances, would accept occasional failure as part of learning, and would be able to talk honestly with others. As an approach that emphasizes trust, concern, empathy, and sensitivity to the whole person, humanistic psychology can become a good foundation for your teacher identity.

Unlike educational researchers in the 1950s and 1960s who focused on highly technical methods of instruction, psychometric testing, and clinical research settings, Rogers was interested in real people doing real things in real contexts. In education, he emphasized the people and attitudes of teaching, not the experiments and statistics. In fact, he cared little for the *products* of learning and focused instead on the *process* of facilitating human growth. Since we live in a complicated, ever-changing world, what is needed is not facts and equations so much as *learning how to learn* and how to move oneself toward "wholeness" as a person.

Several key principles about teaching emerge from Rogers's humanistic theories. Rogers argued—as did John Dewey before him—that humans possess a natural inclination toward learning, but only if the learning is seen as relevant and authentic by students. This encourages

TEXTBOX 5.2

Let us not forget the character Stuart Little in E. B. White's (1945) children's book of the same name. During one of his adventures, Stuart offers to substitute-teach in a school, but the superintendent asks him how he is going to take care of classroom management; Stuart is, after all, a tiny mouse. Confidently, Stuart replies, "I'll make the work interesting and the discipline will take care of itself." That's a good (though incomplete, of course) answer for the rest of us as well.

teachers to find ways to make the material interesting and relevant to students' own lives.

Rogers also believed that people don't learn very well when there's discomfort present. Instead, children and adults learn better when they feel comfortable, supported, and trusted. This means that external threats such as harsh critique, personal attacks, or an atmosphere of fear should be avoided in the classroom. Recall how Liz in Chapter 3 recounted how her girlfriend grew to hate school because she was always being harshly corrected for her pronunciation and grammar. As teachers, part of what we can do is present information and develop activities in ways that increase students' self-esteem, guide students into their own learning, and invite them into *productive* (not destructive) knowledge conflicts that lead to growth and new understandings. This idea is similar to linguist and education researcher Stephen Krashen's (1987) notion of the *affective filter* (introduced in Chapter 3): his hypothesis that language learners have a harder time with their own learning if the educational environment is making them emotionally uncomfortable.

Rogers described successful teachers in humanistic terms. Good teachers are "real" (that is, genuine, authentic, and honest); they emphasize trust and respect with students; they develop caring understandings of students; they're open-minded. Being "real" as a teacher, for Rogers, meant focusing more on the process of becoming fully functioning than on the products of predetermined, fixed curricular goals. Rogers is urging us to trust that young people have the capacity to develop to their full human potential with our help. As teachers, we can create the conditions for this and lead students into their own processes of holistic growth and human development. Humanistic teaching doesn't mean accepting all student responses as equal or any answer as correct, but allowing students to know that they are heard and understood. Students will inevitably rise or fall to the level of expectation we hold for them. Teachers should also recognize that corrections, respectful debate, and supportive probing for clarification are part of the process of student self-growth.

Finally, humanistic psychology suggests that teachers should develop an empathetic understanding of students, striving to find ways to get to know their students and trying to see the world through each student's eyes: "The attitude of standing in the other's shoes, of viewing the world through the student's eyes, is almost unheard of in the classroom. One could listen to thousands of ordinary classroom interactions without coming across one instance of clearly communicated, sensitively accurate, empathic understanding. But it has tremendous releasing effects when it occurs" (Rogers 1969, 112).

This is very important in teaching. Your ability to understand your students, to empathize with them and their perspectives, is necessary if you are going to offer them valuable, relevant, interesting lessons and activities. What might this actually look like in your classroom? Inviting your students to decorate the classroom with you; allowing them to bring in posters, artwork, and other objects from their own lives; paying close attention to how the conditions of your classroom invite free thought and individual expression (not just obeying

Students will inevitably rise or fall to the level of expectation we hold for them.

school rules and predetermined instruction). It's important to allow your students to see you as a real person who becomes joyful and excited about learning new things. Whether we are teaching five-year-olds, fifteen-year-olds, or fifty-five-year-olds, designing learning activities in which students find their own ways into preselected topics and then explore the content in relation to their own lives is crucial. Humanistic psychology reminds us to always consider how the conditions of learning in our classroom can encourage and motivate students (not just us teachers) and must be for all students (not just some).

Humanism also promotes a focus not only on students but also on the *teacher's* own process of achieving full functioning status. We are all still in the process of becoming, and Rogers wanted to remind us of that. He stressed that we, too, need encouraging conditions in order to grow. Just as students need an environment that's both comfortable and challenging, and that is self-directed (not only ends-justified), so, too, do teachers need working conditions that are self-fulfilling and respectful and that lead participants up the arc of their own learning. Be sure to attend to your own learning contexts and do what you can to maximize the conditions of your own professional growth—choosing a compatible school to teach in, befriending thoughtful colleagues, and pursuing your own interests. See Book 6, which focuses on the conditions for successful careers in education.

**Cross-Reference
See Book 6,
which focuses
on the
conditions for
successful
careers in
education.**

HARNESSING YOUR PERSONALITY IN YOUR TEACHING

The tenets of humanistic psychology require that teachers consciously consider the daily role that their personalities play in their teaching, since a teacher's whole person is often implicated in her work. Using your personality in teaching can be an exciting aspect of your education work. What's important is not to let this process go un-acknowledged. If the role of your personality in your teaching is left unrecognized, your personality will probably carry both benefits and detriments for your students. Adopting a teacher-identity approach demands that you pay close, honest attention to the pluses and minuses of the parts of your personality that impact your daily planning and appear in your teaching. This won't always be easy, or fun. On the contrary, it may be painful. For example, you may have to recognize that your sharp, sometimes sarcastic sense of humor that family and friends enjoy may very well hurt the feelings of, and perhaps disempower, some of your students. In fact, an educator who has worked in the United States and on three other continents once mentioned to me that he has seen teacher sarcasm negatively impact more students, regardless of cultural background, than all other negative teacher behaviors combined.

Perhaps you can benefit from some sustained reflection on how you react to high noise levels and chaos in life. This might reveal new dimensions of your approach to classroom management, such as whether you become anxious or uncomfortable when multiple, frenetic conversations occur simultaneously in your classroom. Is such a situation the students' fault, or could it be more about your own tolerance for disorder? Noticing this about yourself may mean that you need to become more tolerant of the discomfort that arises during these situations, since your professional self knows that although energetic students working together can be loud—and can seem unruly—this is often a sign of authentic learning in children. But, then again, perhaps some of your students, too, become distracted by noise and chaos in the classroom. Perhaps it would be helpful for you to candidly explain to students that you personally have a hard time with noise and chaos in the classroom, even though you know it sometimes makes for engaged learning. Naming it and being explicit about it with students can pave the way for compromise. Maybe you can invent a signal or word to use when the noise level is making you uneasy, and students will know to lower the volume.

Nancy, a high-school teacher I've quoted earlier in this book, told me this:

> The bad parts of me show up in my teaching sometimes. I like things to be controlled, and I like to have control. In my classroom, I need to have everyone in a circle, everyone doing what they're supposed to be doing. If they're not, it drives me crazy. That's my own thing— it's not their problem. I'll find myself jumping on a kid who, it turns out, is just getting a piece of paper out of his bag or something. I'm strict in my classroom—it's an academic environment. Part of that makes sense, but part is just that I like to have control in my room. I know that, and talk to students about it. Also, some teachers swear with their students, or use lots of slang. Or talk with students like they're their buddies. I'm not necessarily opposed to that. But that's just not me. I care about academic language. I'm still silly in the classroom, and joke around with them, and let them know about my personal life. But somehow it's different. For example, I don't let students use my first name.

Another common aspect of teachers' personalities that emerges in the classroom is their sense of humor. Laughter in the classroom can be great: it creates some fun and authenticity within learning; it strengthens personal relationships; it reveals a teacher's humanness. But if you're going to use humor, do so carefully. Avoid jokes that come at students' expense. Avoid sarcasm and mocking. Don't tell jokes that rely on stereotypes, culture, or biology for their meaning. Make fun of yourself, not others. Pay close attention to *all* the students' reactions, and always check in afterward with any student whose feelings you believe might have been hurt or who perhaps didn't understand the joke. Don't allow students to make fun of each other unless it's mutually understood to be in good taste. And remember, you're not there for attention or applause, but for the sole benefit of your students' learning and personal growth. Over time, you'll find your own natural yet appropriate teacher's sense of humor.

There are likely many other dimensions to your personality that are actively shaping your teaching. You have a unique set of personal dispositions—combinations of things such as your degree of reflectiveness, your comfort with uncertainty or experimentation, your organizational skills or their absence, your level of extroversion/introversion, and how you typically cope with adversity.

Since there's no single "best" way to be a teacher, you must fashion a successful professional self out of the traits you possess. This is not to lament that you're one kind of person or another: "Gosh, I sure wish I could perform and be funny in the classroom like Ms. So-and-so." Or, "Shoot, I'll never be as universally loved as Mr. Such-and-such." And it's not to conclude that you cannot teach well because you don't have a particular kind of personality that you believe is well suited to teaching. It would be a mistake for you to try to be like those other teachers instead of capitalizing on your own best traits. In the end, students connect with and respect authentic teachers who are knowledgeable, who are passionate about what they do, and who work hard to make learning enjoyable and worthwhile.

Acknowledging your personality characteristics isn't about limiting yourself but about realistically working

TEXTBOX 5.3

I appreciate psychologist Gordon Allport's work on personality dispositions. He defined *personal dispositions* as concrete, easily recognizable consistencies in our behaviors: for example, shyness, altruism, wildness, or selfishness (Allport 1968).

Focus point

with the attributes you possess in service of your goals and your students' success. *This is an exciting part of teacher development: looking candidly at yourself and figuring out how to employ your personality as part of your version of the "perfect teacher."* With creative teacher-identity reflection, you can reframe perceived weaknesses as teaching strengths instead. Your hobbies and personal interests will inevitably carry over and become parts of your professional practice. Acknowledge this and become certain that you're translating your own interests into productive learning practices, not ones that exclude students or impose a particular ideology on them.

Randy, the third-grade teacher quoted earlier, told me how his passions are part of his teacher self:

> It sounds like a bumper sticker, but you must be passionate. In some ways being a good teacher is about finding and translating your passions. Showing kids your passions, letting them see you be passionate about things. For example, I have a boulangerie in my classroom, right over there. I teach the children how to bake bread and they do this with their classmates on their birthdays—it's better than moms bringing in cupcakes. The kids can see my passions and they can join me in them or at least recognize them as passions and say, "Oh, that's Mr. B going crazy over words." And I do. I love the roots of words; I want to marinate the children in words and their meanings; I want them to love poetry! They know I'm passionate about this. These children might think I'm a little crazy, but that's fine with me. I tell them to find their own things to be crazy about.

TEACHING IS EMOTIONAL WORK

Another area to explore in developing your teacher identity is your emotions and their impact on your teaching self. Though emotions and teaching haven't received a lot of research attention in education, they have received some. Topics examined include the emotional disappointments of reform-minded teachers (Little 1996; Huberman 1993), emotions and teacher effectiveness (Haberman 1990; Zehm and Kottler 1993), the emotions of social justice teaching (Chubbuck and Zembylas 2008), and even why research on emotions in teaching is so limited and what can be done about it (Sutton and Wheatley 2003).

When education researcher Andy Hargreaves investigated the emotional dimensions of successful teachers, he found that they were "emotional, passionate beings who connect with their students and fill their work and their classes with pleasure, creativity, challenge, and joy" (Hargreaves 1998, 835). Drawing upon sociology and social psychology, Hargreaves described the relationship between teaching and emotions in terms of four themes:

- Teaching is an emotional practice.
- Teaching and learning involve emotional understanding.
- Teaching is a form of emotional labor.
- Teachers' emotions are inseparable from their moral purposes and their ability to achieve those purposes.

Let's look at those in some detail. As an *emotional practice*, teaching "activates, colors, and expresses teachers' own feelings" and in turn influences the emotional responses of their colleagues and students (1998, 838). This means that teaching is not just technical or intellectual work but is also fundamentally emotional. Teaching also relies on degrees of *emotional understanding:* relationships with students and other adults can be emotional and require emotional sensitivity if they are to be productive. Likewise, emotional misunderstandings can interfere with a teacher's ability to teach his students. In other words, the more emotionally aware a teacher is, the better able he is to recognize and tend to the emotional contours of his relationships with students, colleagues, and supervisors. Interestingly, Hargreaves found that gaps in emotional understanding can widen when teachers come from cultural or class backgrounds different from those of their students. Emotions are not only complex, but may also be culturally influenced.

Teaching is a caring profession that requires a form of *emotional labor*. What this means is that teaching is sometimes emotional, vulnerable work. This can be seen as both a positive and a negative aspect of teaching. "Emotional labor is an important part of teaching, and in many ways, a positive one. For many teachers, it is a labor of love." However, "it is also important to recognize that emotional labor also exposes teachers, making them vulnerable when the conditions of and demands on their work make it hard for them to do their 'emotion work' properly" (1998, 840). I hear experienced teachers talk of "growing a thicker skin" or telling newcomers, "Don't let the work get you down." They're speaking about protecting themselves from some of the emotional intensity that regularly accompanies teaching.

Finally, the emotions of teaching are also shaped by the *moral purpose* inherent in teaching and teachers' professional goals. Failing to live up to one's own moral purpose as an educator can create grief or guilt and become emotionally distressing. And the opposite is true: fulfilling one's moral goals as a teacher can lead to increased happiness and fulfillment in the profession. In this, teaching is considered to be one of those professions in the world in which there is a crucial, moral need. Carrying the weight of the future of your students (and even the future of a society) on the shoulders of your teaching can be intensely emotional. If left alone, it can create emotions such as despair. But if recognized and managed successfully, it can translate into intense satisfaction, high-quality teaching, and hopefulness.

In his study, Hargreaves found—perhaps not surprisingly—that "teachers' emotional commitments and connections to students energized and articulated everything these teachers did: including how they taught, how they planned, and the structures in which they preferred to teach" (1998, 850). This means that we ignore the various roles of our emotions in our practice at our own peril. But how, specifically, should we treat and reflect on our emotions within teaching?

I believe there are two ways that teacher identity helps us with the connection between teaching and emotions. One is by pointing us toward a focus on emotions *in* teaching. This is to say that a teacher's personal emotions and emotional reactions to various experiences and stimuli often intertwine with their pedagogical practices and with their interactions with students. At its heart, there's nothing problematic about that. But your emotions in teaching should not be left unexamined. If, as this chapter has attempted to argue, teaching is built out of personal relationships and humanness, then the emotional dimensions of teaching and learning must be recognized, talked about, and used productively, not destructively.

The second way I view emotions and teaching is to highlight the emotions *of* teaching. This is about the fact that teaching itself can be emotional work—it creates and

---

TEXTBOX 5.4

Let's detach the topic of *emotions and teaching* from historical views of teaching as predominantly women's work, or teacher as mere nurturer. Such linkages deprofessionalize teaching, insult women, and cheapen the value of acknowledging the presence of emotions in education. Instead, a teacher-identity focus frames teachers as whole persons engaged in high-quality professional work and encourages treatment of emotions as part of the holistic interrelatedness of all dimensions of a teacher, whether male or female. A teacher's emotions are one piece of a complicated puzzle, yet every piece of that puzzle impacts students on a daily basis.

heightens various feelings in teachers. Teaching can be stressful at times and can entail feelings of guilt, sadness, disappointment, or despair. Alternatively, it can be positively sublime and lead to feelings of joy, happiness, pride, and hopefulness. A teacher-identity focus opens up the possibility for you to reflect on some of the emotions that teaching stirs in you, and can to some degree guide you in consciously addressing and managing those emotions. As a result you can learn to teach in ways that increase positive feelings for you and your students. But attending to the emotions of your teaching requires acknowledging them first.

The Role of Emotions in Your Teacher Identity

It's not hard to imagine how any one emotion or some combination of them might play out in your teaching on certain days. For example, whether it's their first year of teaching or their twentieth, something many teachers talk about is the potent mix of fear and happiness that accompanies the first day of class each year. We all experience a combination of anxiety and excitement when we meet our class for the first time. Will they like me? Will I like them? Will my comfort as a classroom leader suddenly abandon me? How nice for all of us to have a fresh start! I suggest that you accept and celebrate these feelings; they're an exciting part of the teaching cycle. This is vibrant, meaningful work, and it's only natural to feel both excited and nervous as you begin a new year. You may even want to share these emotions with your new students. It might put them at ease (perhaps they're feeling something similar), it will humanize you in their eyes, and it may lessen your own nervousness simply by virtue of naming it.

Another way that emotions affect teaching is that students will inspire certain emotions in you that influence how you respond to and treat those students (or other students). This is tricky because, as already mentioned, the personal relationships in the classroom or school are key to successful teaching and learning. Your goal should always be to attempt to conjure up the positive, productive emotions with students (such as surprise and happiness) and contain or siphon off the negative ones (such as anger and contempt). I suspect we all know what it's like to suddenly feel angry at one student or a whole class. And sometimes it's unavoidable. What is important, however, is for you to notice a potentially harmful emotion at its onset (or before), identify its source, and quickly decide how *not* to act on it. It doesn't benefit anyone for students to see your anger, contempt, or disgust—and once they see it, depending on the group, they might even try to make it a game among themselves to produce it again.

One recommendation is to spend some time when you are not in the classroom considering students' reactions to your planned classroom activities, discussions, and topics—as well as your own reactions when certain events transpire, controversial beliefs surface, or challenging comments emerge. Outside the teaching situation you may want to identify, predict, and even role-play possible emotionally laden circumstances with colleagues or in your teacher-preparation courses. What triggers your own emotions, and what does it feel like when the emotions first appear? What will you do to redirect or replace those negative emotions with positive responses instead—such as honest and thoughtful comments, a deep breath, or a brief classroom activity that affords you five minutes to regroup? Play out possible scenarios in your head while carpooling to school or sitting on the bus. Develop and write down a few different plans of action that you can employ when necessary—and perhaps fasten that page inside your classroom desk drawer to look at in the heat of the moment. As you become a more experienced teacher, you will have encountered more and more of the possible emotions in teaching—and the situations that trigger them—and so you'll be better able to acknowledge and address them before negative emotions cause trouble. Early in your career, you can easily be jolted into unfamiliar territory that triggers, for example, fear or anger—so be prepared.

If you're teaching a lesson that you expect will lead to a heated discussion about, say, gender, immigration, or politics, you should expect that emotions will run high. Students may be parroting opinions or prejudices coming from parents or grandparents. A student may be intentionally trying to rile you for effect. Perhaps some students are trying out new, half-formed ideas and honestly aren't sure what they believe, or how to articulate their thoughts in productive ways. And it's also likely that several students don't share your personal views on the topic. Anticipate these scenarios; play them out ahead of time; identify the kinds of emotional and pedagogical reactions you hope to exhibit. You should also plan some kind of introductory discussion or activity to acknowledge that the topic might produce strong feelings among students; this will give them a structure and some interpersonal tools to use in dealing with those emotions in productive ways in the classroom. Everyone gains in proactive and honest discussions like these. (John Gaughan's [2001] book *Reinventing English: Teaching in the Contact Zone* prepares secondary-school teachers for emotionally and politically difficult classroom conversations.)

I tell student teachers that when a comment or behavior suddenly makes the classroom dynamic heated and tense, there are a few productive ways to react. If you're prepared for it, you may wish to suspend the formal lesson and treat this new situation as a "teaching moment" of its own. Without focusing on the student whose comment initiated this moment (because that kind of blame often causes defensiveness), address the comments—or better yet, the underlying logic of the comments—and have a conversation about the perspectives or beliefs related to the dustup. Ask questions that encourage students to dig below the surface and identify the clash of perspectives that gave rise to the present conflict. Don't lecture them on what the "right" view or behavior is; instead, facilitate a conversation that encourages students to deconstruct for themselves what's going on. Is it an ethical disagreement about competing belief systems? Is it a legitimate political debate on which opposing sides can reasonably disagree? Is it a conflict between a collective good (such as keeping the schoolyard free of litter) and an individual's freedom ("I can litter if I want; it's a free country!")? Is it perhaps about a personal conflict outside of class between students that is rearing its head inside your lesson today?

Again, it's important to take the pressure off the particular student who initiated the conversation—you don't want to make him or her feel fearful or singled out—and instead reframe it as an interesting, useful topic for discussion. Perhaps tell a personal anecdote about how your own views have changed and grown over time. You could initiate a pedagogical activity, such as "Four Corners." Or, you could quickly create some kind of reflection assignment for students to complete overnight and bring with them—such a move not only gives them time and an activity to deepen their thinking

TEXTBOX 5.5 FOUR CORNERS

Designate each corner of the room as one of the competing positions in question. Ask students to go stand in the corner that best represents their view (no in-between positions allowed!), and invite them one at a time to articulate and defend their views. Encourage students to move from one corner to another as their opinions change or to move to another corner to show understanding by defending that position. Conclude by offering or summarizing some useful ways to frame the debate and celebrating students' willingness to shift positions as the conversation deepened.

but also gives you a chance to reflect on the topic; you can then return to it the next day better prepared.

All of this is helpful if you're prepared for a sudden, emotionally loaded teaching moment. But what if you aren't ready for it? In that case, you're better off pausing the lesson that was under way, acknowledging what has just happened, making a general comment or two about it, and then telling students that you'd like everyone to think about what has been said or what has just occurred, and that the group will return to it in the next class meeting or the next day to discuss it. This approach has several benefits. One is that it gives you time to diagnose what happened and how you want to handle it, instead of having to act on the fly. The time lapse offers the students themselves a chance to cool down and prepare to reengage in the topic at a time when they can do it intellectually, not just emotionally. The third benefit is that it creates some distance between the event and the student who initiated it, making it easier for you to frame the event as a clash of ideas that can be considered and addressed rather than a personal response to a specific student.

All this is not, of course, to advocate some kind of ethical relativism. All views and practices in life are not morally equal. You should not accept every opinion your students put forward. There are better and worse, admirable and deplorable ways to live a life, and many ideas and social practices can rightly be condemned in a modern democracy such as ours. If you are not sure about how to handle a sensitive topic in class or need advice on an explosive discussion that occurred, then be sure to talk with several of your colleagues who might be able to help you navigate the issue with sensitivity. As a teacher you've been entrusted not only with the task of guiding students toward academic and intellectual growth but also with the privilege of helping them understand and embody the democratic values of our society. You shouldn't shirk that moral purpose of teaching.

That said, however, lecturing to students dogmatically about wrong and right, and singling out students who disagree with you—or with the bulk of the class—for humiliation or abject punishment are not practices aligned with the constructivist views of teaching that I advocate.

Teacher Burnout

Some teachers experience chronic negative emotions, and this is frequently due to the conditions of their work. Research has documented the frequency of teacher burnout. **Teacher burnout** is a persistent sense of exhaustion, hopelessness, or powerlessness that decreases one's effectiveness and satisfaction with teaching—and can lead to a departure from the profession. Walter Gmelch (1983) prefers the term "rustout" to burnout because it's more indicative of the slow, corrosive nature of the process. Teachers sometimes report elevated levels of stress, attributing them to the demands of their work and a perceived lack of control over their daily activities. And many educators and researchers lament the amount of "overwork"—the excessive time demands on schoolteachers. Overwork is nevertheless inherent to many teaching assignments, especially in urban, failing, or underfunded schools. It is important to learn how to manage these negative emotions.

Key concept
teacher burnout

These states of emotional frustration are akin to the occupational stress found in other lines of work. Researcher Yvonne Gold (1993) believes that teacher burnout results from two sources: the teacher's personality and the workplace conditions. She found that risk factors for burnout included the young and inexperienced, those whose parents were achievement-oriented, and people who tended to be alone frequently. Working conditions found to contribute to teacher burnout include little or no opportunities for collaboration, working days governed by strict scheduling and the constant ringing of

**Cross-Reference
This concept
connects to
other books in
this series,
especially Books
3, 4, and 6.**

bells, and a lack of autonomy in one's daily work. Some of these factors are organizational conditions of schools that are in need of wholesale reform: many educational reformers spend their careers attempting to make schools better suited for teacher retention and for high-quality teaching and learning. This concept connects to other books in this series, especially Books 3, 4, and 6.

Some of these factors are beyond your control, but others are things that you can adjust. At the end of Chapter 6, I write more directly about what you can do to improve your working conditions, teacher effectiveness, and identity disposition within the contemporary educational landscape. But some factors related to teacher stress can be addressed by pursuing exactly the opposite of what causes burnout. If one factor of burnout is loneliness, be sure to find professional allies and spend sufficient time with friends. If you lack opportunities for professional collaboration, seek to create ways for teachers at your school to collaborate, even if it takes dogged persistence to do so. If your personality characteristics are not a good match for the school where you are working, find work in a school that fits your particular teacher-identity contours. And, of course, every teacher should pursue common stress-reduction strategies such as relaxing often, sleeping sufficiently, eating nutritiously, exercising regularly, and managing time efficiently. I often recommend that beginning teachers choose one weekend day every week during which they promise not to do any schoolwork. This can be a hard promise to keep, but it's a necessary step for teachers to take in order to preserve the stamina and emotional balance they need to get through an entire school year (and it helps to preserve one's personal relationships).

SELF-EFFICACY

Teacher identity concerns itself with the question, *Who am I as a teacher?* Part of any reflection on "Who am I?"

must logically include subquestions such as "What am I good at?" "Are my abilities a good match for my profession?" "Will I be successful?" So your own bundle of identity-related understandings *of* and *about* yourself as a teacher surely includes questions about confidence, self-esteem, and self-efficacy related to teaching. Such questions are worth considering because your perceptions of your own likelihood of success as a teacher actually do influence your teaching. Self-efficacy is concerned with people's perceptions of their abilities to be successful: your perceptions of your abilities produce actual effects in terms of the attitudes and angles of approach you bring to the work.

Bandura's Self-Efficacy and Teaching

The concept of self-efficacy is part of a social-cognitive theory outlined, most notably, by psychologist Albert Bandura. It's related to but different from the notion of "self-esteem."

Self-efficacy refers to a person's own sense of his or her ability to do things successfully. More technically, Bandura describes it as the set of "beliefs in one's capabilities to organize and execute the courses of action required to manage prospective situations" (Bandura 1995, 2).

TEXTBOX 5.6

Self-esteem is typically considered an enduring personality characteristic or temporary disposition relating to a person's evaluation of himself or herself. It includes general opinions—such as "I'm a good person" or "I am proud of myself"—as well as narrower evaluations—such as "I have a good memory for faces, but not names" or "I did well today." That's different from self-efficacy.

In his research, Bandura found a positive correlation between perceived self-efficacy and what individuals actually do: higher self-efficacy leads to a higher sense of optimism and aptitude when approaching difficult tasks, while a lower sense of self-efficacy may lead someone to approach tasks believing that they're more difficult than in fact they are. The degree of a person's belief that he or she *can be* successful guides the person's subsequent actions in ways that make eventual success more likely and that increase one's willingness to take on challenges. Bandura wrote that "self-efficacy judgments, whether accurate or faulty, influence choice of activities and environmental settings. People avoid activities that they believe exceed their coping capabilities, but they undertake and perform assuredly those that they judge themselves as capable of managing" (1982, 123). Bandura identified four sources of information that people draw on as they form and adjust their sense of self-efficacy: enactive attainments, vicarious experiences, verbal persuasion, and physiological state (see Textbox 5.7).

Personally, I'm not fully convinced of the accuracy of Bandura's theories. They may work better as a loose guide than as proven truth because they might be culturally skewed, methodologically suspect, or overly neat. It's possible that his arrows of causality are going the wrong way (maybe success leads to confidence more than confidence leads to success) or are double-sided (each reciprocally influencing the other). But, whether we accept it as proven fact or simply as useful procedure, applied to education the concept of self-efficacy carries value and offers important suggestions for your teacher identity. For example, at the beginning of her teacher-preparation experience, Liz told me that she didn't believe that a single year of university teacher education could provide enough training for someone to teach well, but that it offered her "the illusion of confidence . . . and that will probably be enough to make me feel like I'm doing okay. It's probably a façade or something I would convince my-

TEXTBOX 5.7 SOURCES OF A PERSON'S SELF-EFFICACY

ENACTIVE ATTAINMENTS. Having success in a given task increases one's sense of self-efficacy around it, whereas repeated failure lowers it. In other words, the more you do something successfully, the more confident you will become about doing it.

VICARIOUS EXPERIENCES. Seeing "similar others" perform well positively influences one's own sense of self-efficacy. In other words, watching others complete a task successfully increases your own confidence about being able to complete it. This idea is connected to the concept of "modeling" in education in which a teacher (or teacher-educator) exhibits the behaviors she wants her students to imitate.

VERBAL PERSUASION. Being praised or encouraged by others contributes to successful performance in a limited way: "It can contribute to successful performance if the heightened appraisal is within realistic bounds . . . [and has] greatest impact on people who have some reason to believe that they can produce effects through their actions" (Bandura 1982, 127). In other words, verbal encouragement helps, but only to a certain degree.

PHYSIOLOGICAL STATE. One's physical state influences a person's sense of self-efficacy. For example, Bandura found that people are less likely to expect success when they feel tense or agitated. This connects to the earlier point made by Carl Rogers (and Stephen Krashen) that a learner's physical or psychological comfort level is related to his or her ability to learn (or in this case feel confident).

self of. I think that in most respects performance is based on confidence. If you think you're good at a thing, then that will be enough to stand on, at least in the beginning." That is self-efficacy.

One use of the concept of self-efficacy for us here is that it highlights the interconnectedness among a teacher's prior experiences, professional preparation, confidence, abilities, teaching practices, and future career predictions. All these components of a teacher's life are in conversation with each other. And this iterative notion of a teacher's self-beliefs, professional perspectives, and teaching approach being interconnected brings us back to teacher identity—specifically, your teacher identity. I recommend that you carefully consider how your personal history has shaped your level of confidence as a teacher. Are you typically particularly hard on yourself (and, if so, might you want to let up a little)? Or do you often underestimate your talents (and, if so, would you benefit from reminding yourself about what you're good at)? When you're feeling a lack of confidence professionally, emphasize the things you know you're good at. Draw on your successes and your strengths as you take on new challenges. For example, if you happen to be a talented musician, bring that into the classroom—and play for your students as part of a lesson every now and then. Or if you're a geography whiz, find a way to occasionally lead a geography game or some other activity that challenges both you and students.

A second use of the concept of self-efficacy in teaching is to remind us that we (and our students) rise or fall to the levels of our own expectations. Expect great teaching from yourself and you'll be primed to deliver it. In the same vein, your expectations of students will likely shape how they see themselves in the classroom. This means that it is important to enact careful, conscious, productive interactions with students. Part of your job is to attend to their own processes of self-efficacy. Earlier in this chapter I invoked Carl Rogers to suggest that students must feel comfortable at school if they are going to engage in learning. Trust must be established. Now we can add that your interactions with students will also have an

> **TEXTBOX 5.8**
>
> *Modeling* is a common term in psychology, sociology, and neuroscience. Though there are differences in how it is used in these disciplines, the term generally describes the process by which a person (or animal) learns by imitating others, especially the practices of the "model"—such as a parent or teacher—who exhibits behaviors to be learned. In teaching it refers to the act of teachers performing behaviors that their students will pick up. One can model desirable or undesirable behaviors; one's modeling can be intentional or not. Advocates of modeling encourage teachers to find successful techniques for doing it; critics worry that modeling is overly behavioristic and encourages mere mimicry.

effect on their developing views of their abilities. Use that power carefully, and never unthinkingly.

Randy, the third-grade teacher, told me that he views his job as largely about uncovering the abilities inherent in students:

> Finding the talent in my students is a big part of my job. The first month I probe and find out indirectly and directly at least one thing that each child does well. And then I have to let this child know that I know that information. I do it by talking with them, laughing with them, joking with them, having lunch with them, or during informal conversations on the yard. The chairs in my classroom are low, so I spend a lot of time on the floor—to be at eye level. It needs to be sharing though, so that it's not the teacher always drilling for information but also the teacher sharing his or her own stuff with them. We celebrate the talents of each other.

Some studies of self-efficacy have been applied to teaching directly. A. E. Woolfolk and W. K. Hoy (1990) found that teachers' sense of self-efficacy affected their general orientation toward education practices. They found that teachers with "a low sense of instructional efficacy" tended to be more controlling of students than those with a high sense of self-efficacy and that they used reward and punishment more frequently in order to get students to study. Conversely, they found that teachers who believed strongly in their own efficacy as instructors tended to stress the intrinsic rewards of learning and to emphasize self-directedness. Others, such as P. T. Ashton and R. B. Webb (1986), found positive correlations between teachers' perceived self-efficacy and their students' achievement. Again, I'm not offering these ideas as facts because I am not fully convinced of the efficacy of self-efficacy research. As a set of helpful hints about success, however, self-efficacy offers food for thought for both teachers and teacher-educators.

CONCLUSION

A teacher's professional identity is composed of personal, humanistic elements as much as formal, technical skills and specialized knowledge. I do not wish to instigate any kind of battle about which side carries more weight. Successful teaching is both a personal, often emotional set of productive human relationships and a product of specialized knowledge, rigorous training, and proved methods. My point is that one domain cannot succeed without the other. Your teacher identity is an active collection of both, and therefore you must pay attention to the personal, "human" sides of your teacher self as well as the professional, technical sides. And as the next chapter shall demonstrate, your political, racial, and cultural sides are an active part of your teacher identity, too.

DISCUSSION QUESTIONS

1. How would family and friends describe your general personality? How would you describe your personality?

2. What aspects of your personality do you want to include in your professional identity? Which aspects do you think you should leave out of it?

3. Can you think of examples in your own schooling where a teacher's care, concern, trust, and compassion were powerful parts of the experience for you? What was this like? Conversely, can you think of examples where a teacher's lack of concern, or downright antipathy, had a powerful effect on you? What was that like?

4. What, generally, triggers your own strong emotions, and what does it feel like when those emotions first appear? What will you do to redirect or replace those negative emotions in the classroom with positive responses instead?

5. How will you address your fears or perceived professional insecurities in your teaching and/or reframe them as positive aspects instead?

FURTHER READING

Csikszentmihalyi, M. 2008. *Flow: The Psychology of Optimal Experience*. New York: HarperPerennial Modern Classics.

Gmelch, W. H. 1983. "Stress for Success: How to Optimize Your Performance." *Theory into Practice* 22, no. 1: 7–14.

Hargreaves, A. 1995. *Changing Teachers, Changing Times: Teachers' Work and Culture in the Postmodern Age*. London: Cassell.

Tremmel, R. 1993. "Zen and the Art of Reflective Practice in Teacher Education." *Harvard Educational Review* 63, no. 4: 434–458.

Zehm, S., and J. Kottler. 1993. *On Being a Teacher: The Human Dimension*. Newbury Park, CA: Corwin Press.

CHAPTER SIX

THE POLITICAL DIMENSIONS OF TEACHING AND IDENTITY

When I first began teaching, I thought that a teacher gets up there and lectures. I knew my subject, I was going to lecture and use the textbook, and give tests. I was going to be fun and young and funny—and students were going to be into it, and love me! But then I got started teaching and realized how much of me and my own history was wrapped up in what I thought a teacher was. My own personal stuff is all wrapped up in my teaching, and I needed to find a way to figure all that out. My politics, my views of people and the world, my biases. So many teachers are teaching their own personal belief systems. And I don't know if that bothers me or not. I guess it's good and it's bad. But what scares me is when teachers don't realize they're doing it.

> —Nancy, a ninth-year California high-school social-science teacher

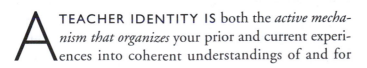

TEACHER IDENTITY IS both the *active mechanism that organizes* your prior and current experiences into coherent understandings of and for yourself as an educator and the *actual, resulting bundle* of those experiences and understandings. It's both the process and the product of your ongoing teacher development. This is why it warrants the kind of attention this book advocates. Early chapters examined how teachers' past, their entry into the profession, and their professional preparation reciprocally create their teacher identities. Middle chapters investigated identity influences on teacher practice, including embedded roles of biography, emotions, and personality dispositions. This final chapter addresses the *cultural and political dimensions of teacher identity* and concludes with a look at the current policy climate of teaching in public K–12 schools. With these topics, I hope to bring to a close our extended conversation about teacher identity by focusing on the teaching you will do tomorrow. If the book began with histories of teaching, it can conclude by pointing out that you are teaching's future.

First, I outline a way for you to conduct a teacher-identity inventory in relation to race, culture, power, and social justice. Second, I ask you to consider critical pedagogy: a politicized view of education as an ongoing struggle between oppression and liberation. I close with a look at the contemporary policy culture of schooling in the United States in order to contextualize how you can be the teacher in today's classrooms that you desire to be, and that your students need you to be.

RACE, CLASS, CULTURE, AND POWER— AND YOUR TEACHER IDENTITY

The Race, Culture, and Power Inventory[1]

Chapter 4 discussed a method for taking inventory of your personal history in order to examine how your past shapes your present and suggested ways to make necessary adjustments. This section offers something similar but with a focus on race, class, gender, power, culture, and language, because who you are and the kinds of personal experiences you have lived are intimately tied to how you've been shaped vis-à-vis race, class, gender, and many other cultural dimensions. That much may seem obvious. But an explicit focus on topics of oppression and liberation, discrimination and privilege, and the role of power in teaching is often neglected or mishandled because it's a difficult conversation to broach. Talking about ways in which—for example—the color of our skin, our religious orientation, or our sexual identity might afford us special privileges or deny us equal rights poses emotional, political, and linguistic challenges.

For one thing, many of us don't often find ourselves in mixed company in settings where we can talk openly and honestly about discrimination and privilege. If we are honest, then we probably will find that, too often, "birds of a feather flock together." In other words, many people spend much of their personal time with like-minded folks. As a result, many of us have a false sense that everyone more or less shares a common worldview—our worldview—which in turn lends a kind of self-confirming character to the conversations and perspectives of the groups we are in. It's hard to confront differences when friends and family, on the surface at least, are mostly similar. In education this is also true. Teachers in a school frequently faction off into like-minded subgroups, whole schools faction off (in the form of charter or private schools) from the larger system, and "shared vision" sometimes becomes a proxy for social segregation.

A second reason that candid conversations around race, culture, and power are rare is that they're difficult to carry out. It's hard to find the words to talk accurately about one's own history of privilege and discrimination (or lack thereof) without lapsing into generalizations, anger, or pathos. It's tricky business to talk about and attempt to characterize other groups of people, other cultural practices, and other belief systems without tripping

Cross-Reference
For a parallel discussion on the difficulty of discussing race and class, see Book 4, Chapter 2.

over deficit views, stereotypes, or misunderstandings. Words, phrases, or even whole conversations can easily get turned and twisted as they're carried out—and are always liable to misinterpretation. It's emotionally difficult to talk about things such as white privilege, social class, racism, or heteronormativity—just to name a few—without tumbling into combinations of defensiveness, guilt, blame, and confusion.

Participants in any conversational setting, whether it's a recreational get-together, a classroom of students, or a teachers' meeting, are often reluctant to engage in potentially heated, emotional, highly personal discussions where relationships could become threatened and identity structures made vulnerable. And we might even be a bit fearful of what these conversations would tell us about ourselves. In his short 2009 essay entitled "We Can't Stop Talking about Race in America," author David Mamet opined that "race, like sex, is a subject on which it is near impossible to tell the truth. In each, desire, self-interest and self-image make the truth inconvenient to share not only with strangers (who may, legitimately or not, be viewed as opponents) but also

TEXTBOX 6.1

The term *heteronormativity* draws attention to the whole social system of the "compulsive heterosexuality" (Rich 1978/1993) and discrimination toward homosexuality that shape (and enforce) human activity in our society. By using this term, we can transcend the shortcomings of more commonly used language. For example, the term *homophobia* focuses attention on fear (and is therefore made to seem almost natural) rather than on systematic oppression. *Heterosexism* does not put enough emphasis on the way that the dominant, heterosexual culture of the United States imposes stereotypes and subjugating practices on persons who are gay, lesbian, bisexual, transgender, or questioning (GLBTQ).

with members of one's own group, and, indeed, with oneself" (Mamet 2009, 12).

For these reasons (and many others), beginning teachers are rarely offered the chance to talk deeply about issues of culture and power in supportive settings led by a well-prepared facilitator. Frankly, it's just easier for a teacher-educator or school principal to recommend books or articles for teachers to read and then refer people to printed school policies and state laws, or to repeat bromides about equity and multiculturalism. But that's not enough. Oppression, discrimination, unearned privilege, and power continue to wield undue and unequal influence on our schools, on society, and on our children. There are clear, documented patterns of mistreatment and abuse and woefully inadequate support of certain populations in the United States and around the world.

The majority of teachers in the United States are white Anglos, yet the student population in U.S. schools is increasingly diverse (Banks and Banks 2005; Sleeter 2005, 2007). Debates rage about whether that discrepancy matters, whether it should matter, and what should be done about it. But those are broad debates about policy and other large-scale dimensions of teaching and learning; while not unimportant, they are not the focus of this book. Instead, you are one person with your own set of biological, cultural, ethnic, racial characteristics, and you are (or will be) teaching a set of equally unique human beings. Hopefully, you will take pains to ensure that you have looked closely at your own identity in relation to race, culture, and power—and identified where your own prejudices reside, where they came from, how they're potentially destructive, and how exactly you will replace them with more sensitive, forward-looking, equity-minded teaching perspectives.

Cross-Reference See Book 2, Chapter 2, for more on the importance of understanding diverse cultures and traditions.

Given the continued nature of oppression in U.S. society and schools, it is essential for any educator to do this kind of work. Just as in Chapter 4, where you drew the strands of your own personal history on paper and thought about ways that your "life themes" may have shaped your embedded conceptions of teaching and learning, so, too, should you critically interrogate your cultural, racial, ethnic, gender-based, and power-sensitive history. The sections below offer a teacher-identity focus for how teachers might think about their teaching in relation to race, culture, power, and social justice.

RACIAL IDENTITY DEVELOPMENT. Drawing on work by psychologists and sociologists, Beverly Tatum—a developmental psychologist herself—in her 1997 book *Why Are All the Black Kids Sitting Together in the Cafeteria? And Other Conversations about Race*—outlined some of the processes by which people gradually become aware of their own race and develop their own racial identities. The general point Tatum made was that our race-based understandings of ourselves and others change and grow over time, but only if we actively confront and work on them. This process is "developmental" in the sense that one's forward movement, while neither fully linear nor guaranteed, is a kind of expected growth that's encouraged or impeded by both external factors and our own willingness to engage in the process. If we do nothing, we're liable to become "stuck" at an early stage in the process—a stage in which we feel guilt or defensiveness about our race, for example. But if we talk with others, read the relevant research, and engage in candid, sensitive self-reflection, we're able to mature into increasingly sophisticated and healthy human beings who are both culturally and racially sensitive.

Such a process is important for everyone in life but especially for teachers, since teachers work with young people in potentially intense, life-changing ways and their "core technology"—as it were—exists inside of close relationships with students and families. Some teachers teach students whose cultural identities match their own. That's one thing. Other teachers teach students who are culturally or otherwise very different from them. That's another thing. In both cases, however, teachers have a responsibility to critically examine and thoughtfully adjust their own teacher identities in relation to race, ethnicity, culture, and power—and the particular social characteristics of their students.

It's important to begin the process of political-identity teacher reflection by admitting that we all have prejudices. No matter where one is in the process of becoming the person he or she wants to be, prejudices still exist. Admitting that about yourself takes the pressure off because it eliminates your need to put up defenses and helps others to engage honestly too. As Tatum pointed out, the "smog" of racism is in the air that all of us have breathed our whole lives. It's all right to admit that as we've developed into who we are now, we've been breathing in some smog along with the rest of the air. We can hope that we've expelled most of it from within us. But some surely remains. Acknowledging this both to yourself during reflection and to others during conversation is a useful first step.

TEXTBOX 6.2

Education researcher Philip Jackson (1986) coined the phrase *presumption of shared identity* to refer to teachers assuming that their students are just like them. Teachers who presume shared identity are usually wrong, and relying on a false sense of sameness in the classroom carries potential harm. However, it's also problematic to presume too much distance from your students. They're not another species or genus altogether, and framing yourself as very distant from them carries potential trouble, too. Finding an informed, effective balance is the key. (For more on this topic, see Lisa Delpit's [1995] *Other People's Children: Cultural Conflict in the Classroom*, Cristina Igoa's [1995] *The Inner World of the Immigrant Child*, and Gloria Ladson-Billings's [1994] *The Dreamkeepers: Successful Teachers of African American Children*.)

So, reading books on the topic is essential. So, too, is engaging in personal reflection, conversations with family members and colleagues, and professional discussions similar to those that I recommended in Chapter 4, but with a focus this time on issues of race, class, culture, and power.

YOUR RACIAL AND CULTURAL AUTOBIOGRAPHY. To give shape to your race and culture inventory, I recommend writing your autobiography. Years ago, education professor Madeleine Grumet (1994) wrote an article entitled "Reading the Relations of Teaching." I'm oversimplifying here, but it's about the fact that beginning teachers, when thinking back on their own lives as students, sometimes underestimate the social nature of their learning and overestimate its individualness. They believe that they more or less taught themselves. In fact, however, Grumet argued, we learn socially. We learn to be literate, learn what it means "to know," or learn how the world works by way of our social interactions with others—family, peers, teachers, and society. To remind oneself of that is a powerful learning experience of its own. If teachers can excavate and learn to reframe some of the social dimensions of their own educational events, their teaching practices may change in ways that benefit their students. The resulting shift in thinking encourages teachers to more explicitly acknowledge and support students' social relationships within the teaching-learning equation, for example, and to adopt commensurately social instructional methods.

Not only does Grumet believe that teachers can learn from reframing social aspects of their prior learning, but she also argues that writing analytically about one's past (as a learner) offers greater potential for teacher reflection than simply keeping a teaching journal. Grumet wrote, "It is critical that autobiographical studies in teacher education not be confined to journals that record the students' teaching experiences. Telling a story does not constitute reflection. Reflexivity requires thinking about your own thought" (Grumet 1994, 255). Grumet assigned her teacher-education students to write their own learning autobiographies and critically analyze them, through their developing teacher lenses, afterward.

Taking a cue from Grumet, I suggest that you write your own autobiography that focuses on your personal history around race, gender, heteronormativity, language use, religion, class, and other dimensions of privilege and oppression. Consider beginning with discussion of your family, other adults in your life during your childhood, and your childhood community. Describe the various events and memories of your early years—when you first began to notice bigotry, social inequality, and other dimensions of "difference." And then take it from there:

- How (and why) have you changed, if at all?
- How do you suppose your history might be shaping your ideas about education and your teaching practice?
- What kind of racially and culturally sensitive educator do you strive to be—and what might currently be obstructing that goal?

It's important that you attend to your own history in a *critical* way. That is, do not merely look with bemused detachment at the various contours of your cultural autobiography, but instead critique yourself. Look for your own bias and discrimination; ferret out various dimensions of your relationship to power, race, and culture that are potentially destructive (to yourself and to your students). Apply perspectives and belief systems different from your own to probe your assumptions or to push yourself to concede some of the things about you that still need work.

Tell your story chronologically—from childhood until now. Ask yourself the hard questions, write down your answers, and ultimately share and talk about your autobiography with others who are engaged in a similar process.

TEXTBOX 6.3   THE POWER OF TEACHING OBSERVATIONS

Having a second set of eyes in your classroom can reveal important characteristics of your teaching. Invite a trusted peer in to observe you teach and ask him to record your interactions with students: With whom do you talk the most? Whom do you call on? Who receives short, clipped responses and who receives longer, more encouraging ones? Are there students you ignore? Ask your peer to record this information with tick marks in columns for boys and girls, students in the front and students in the back of the class, racial and ethnic groups, and so on. The results will help you make sure you're not neglecting anyone or treating some students unfairly.

Analyze what you learn about yourself and make concrete changes to your instructional practices accordingly. Invite colleagues to observe your teaching with a critical (but constructive) eye on your cultural, gendered, and racial practices in the classroom. After you have written your autobiography, use the questions at the end of this chapter to guide your subsequent critical self-reflection.

CRITICAL PEDAGOGY

Critical pedagogy is an approach to education that emphasizes critical issues of race, economics, culture, and power—and advocates a politically radicalized form of teaching practice. At its center is the belief that teaching is always political work and that learning in schools is steeped within oppression and liberation, discrimination and empowerment. Yet its adherents believe that education can be transformed. Critical pedagogy is an apt topic to raise when integrating issues of culture and power into your teacher identity because it offers a helpful, preexisting set of complementary ideas and teaching approaches. (For more information on critical pedagogy, see Darder et al. 2003; Freire 1970, 1985; McLaren and Kincheloe 2007; Shor 1987; Wink 2004.)

Critical pedagogy emerges out of views of education that derive from Marxism and neo-Marxian thought, critical theory, and recent traditions such as multiculturalism, culturally responsive teaching, and social-justice education. Its characteristics include the following:

- From Marxism and neo-Marxian thought, a belief that, in a capitalist system, the ruling class mostly controls society's economic means of production as well as social institutions such as government and schooling.
- From critical theory, a belief that social and cultural institutions (such as the media, marriage, and education) are composed of ideological belief systems—and that therefore, participating in cultural institutions (such as schooling) leads a person to accept their ideologies and to conform to accompanying values and perspectives. Furthermore, participation in the institution reinforces the ideological system it represents.
- A view of schools as frequent sites of oppressive social action, but with the potential to be transformed into more humanizing, liberating, empowering places.
- An emphasis on recognizing how embedded, systematic processes of power and discrimination shape what happens in classrooms—and on working to change those systems.
- A loosely assembled approach to teaching that stresses individual and collective student empowerment through culturally sensitive, political, problem-posing forms of instruction, growth, and activism inside and outside the classroom.

**Cross-Reference
Teaching for
social change is
the focus of
Book 5.**

Critical pedagogy can help support teachers in multiple ways as they develop successful teacher identities. Teacher identity requires that we treat all the complex dimensions in play for any single teacher—and that includes vigilant attention to matters of race, class, culture, and power. You're unique; your own ethnic, racial, gendered background has shaped who you are, but you are not wholly determined by those cultural characteristics. We err if we neglect to consider the embedded, active parts of our professional identities that derive from race, class, gender, and other sociopolitical dimensions. It's rarely easy, but all teachers will benefit from a critical focus on their own teaching self—and, accordingly, a thoughtful adjustment of their professional approach. As Paulo Freire wrote, "Those who authentically commit themselves to the people must re-examine themselves constantly" (1970, 60).

So the first way that critical pedagogy can inform teacher identity is by insisting on this kind of critical self-analysis. A second way is by giving us the constant reminder that we must view every student as unique and full of potential. Each of your students has had various experiences with oppression, privilege, discrimination, and empowerment. Those experiences have a hand in shaping who they're becoming. Acknowledging these complex individual social identities should discourage you from treating students in broad, stereotypical ways. Achieving an effective balance is key. On the one hand, to group students in your mind and in your teaching practices by way of broad strokes such as gender, personality type, race, or ability deprives them of the chance to show you who they really are; it limits their ability to be themselves. You wouldn't want that for yourself as a teacher, and your students don't deserve it either. On the other hand, though, you must not ignore the effects of their sociopolitical and economic characteristics. The world has treated your students in particularized ways that require your sensitivity and that call out for your thoughtful empowerment of each student. Recognize, honor, and build on your students' cultural and racial lived experiences.

Third, an emphasis on identity—the whole person existing inside the lived world, continually growing and changing—underscores the need for teachers to attend to the social, political, moral, and cultural dimensions of the planet in their classrooms. Teaching is indeed always a political act. We shouldn't narrow our vision so much that we think education is just about kids learning academic information in a closed classroom. Participating in a classroom (as a student or a teacher) activates not just intellectual and subject-matter dimensions but also many other aspects of human development: personal relationships, increased or decreased empowerment, redefinitions of oneself in relation to the larger world, and many emotional and psychological responses.

A person's whole identity is invoked in the process of teaching and learning—and so the holistic nature of teacher identity fits nicely. Even though teachers sometimes speak of it this way, a classroom is never really a sealed world of its own. It participates in the larger practices and perspectives of the school, the community, the district, and the world. As they're learning in your classroom, your students are actively using (and revising) views of themselves in relation to power and race, class, gender, and sexuality. They are continually developing their own ideas about what it means to be successful in ways largely informed by their experiences outside the school and with people other than fellow students and their teachers. Critical pedagogy and a teacher-identity perspective encourage teachers to acknowledge and confront those powerful social factors as they design a curriculum, plan lessons, lead classroom activities, and conduct the additional work of teaching. *A successful teacher doesn't only teach reading, writing, and arithmetic, but* teaches the world *in her classroom.*

Focus point

In addition, critical pedagogy isn't limited to what teachers do in the classroom. Like identity, it accepts that boundaries—between work and home, between self and others, between school and the larger world—are blurry or even illusory, if you dig deeply enough. Critical pedagogy therefore implores teachers to extend their work into the larger communities where they live and to seek to effect democratic change in ways big and small, global and local, collective and individual. In Textbox 6.4, I include a list like the one I hand out to students at the end of my undergraduate Critical Pedagogy course. It's not about how to pass the class or even how to be effective teachers once they're in the classroom, but about ways that critical pedagogy might operate as a way of life.

There are myriad ways for you to recognize and refine your own professional identity in relation to the lessons of critical pedagogy. Many teacher-education programs currently have a critical pedagogical focus, though I encourage even more educators and teaching programs to formally include critical pedagogy in the repertoire of teaching models they offer.

THE FUTURE OF YOUR TEACHING

This book has tried to travel a long journey in approximately 160 pages. It began by presenting landscapes of teaching, teacher education, and professional development. It introduced teacher identity as a viable means for integrating teachers' personal biographies with their professional preparation inside the historical and current contexts of their teaching. In doing so, I've tried to offer teacher identity as a tool that you can use to reflect on the teacher you've become thus far, and to better direct the contours of the teacher you are becoming. I illustrated teacher identity by narrating one new teacher's complex experience navigating the travails of beginning teaching. I have also considered the ways in which emotional, psychological, and political aspects enter into anyone's teaching practice—all the while recommending how readers can become more conscious and in more

TEXTBOX 6.4   CRITICAL PEDAGOGY: HOW TO MAKE A DIFFERENCE IN THE WORLD

1. Change yourself. It starts within. Monitor your language use, how you treat others (strangers included), what ideologies you accept for yourself and place onto others.
2. Become a teacher-leader, an education activist, a teacher whose influence extends past the classroom. Never stop learning; continue your critical pedagogy education. Question everything.
3. Get involved in other aspects of education. Help reform teacher education, become a policymaker, become a principal, start a school. Write education articles, blogs, letters to the newspaper. Get active in the community.
4. Get active in a social-justice organization or two. There are lots. Ask around; search the Web. Organize with others to make a difference.
5. Find allies. It's isolating to do this kind of work alone. Hook up with like-minded people and join groups. One receives support, energy, solace, and community from being part of a group. Recruit other individuals into your group.
6. Encourage friends, family, and people you meet to understand the importance of all this. Don't stay silent (and therefore complicit) in the face of oppressive interactions, jokes, practices, or policies. Don't underestimate the effect that language has on identity development. Small details carry big influences.
7. As a parent, citizen, friend, employee, church member, or neighbor, rebuild your own institutions around critical pedagogy principles. Create your family, your relationships, and your communities around humanizing principles. Always speak out against dehumanization.
8. Become an active and knowledgeable voter who always participates in elections, especially those seemingly mundane ones at the local level: that's where differences get made. A responsible citizen learns the details of elections and ballot measures and always votes.

continues

TEXTBOX 6.4   CONTINUED

9. Run for a seat on your local school board.

10. Make your own film about issues you care about. Digital video is cheap and easy. Final Cut Pro allows you to edit on your computer, and there are many local independent film festivals for you to enter as well as online sites on which you can show your film.

11. Be conscious of yourself as a citizen and member of society: choose your news and entertainment sources wisely. Rather than just taking what's easy to find (for example, your TV, CNN.com, or YouTube), seek out alternative news sources such as BBC, *Mother Jones*, the *Utne Reader*, National Public Radio, and Pacifica Radio. Visit the websites of social critics, artists, and activists such as Michael Franti (www.michaelfranti.com), Peter McLaren (www.gseis.ucla.edu/~mclaren/), Kara Walker (www.learn.walkerart.org/karawalker), and Cornel West (www.cornelwest.com).

12. Be a critical consumer who votes with his wallet and shops with his conscience. Don't buy things that are egregiously linked to oppressive practices. Buy products from companies whose business practices and politics you can be proud of. And tell others what you learn about products and politics.

control of how they're developing. All this leaves us squarely at the foot of the door of our own future teaching. I hope that at this point you are asking, "What does all this mean for me now as a teacher?" To begin to answer that question, let's consider the current teaching culture in many U.S. public schools.

THE CURRENT POLICY CLIMATE IN EDUCATION

As complicated as teaching is even under the best of circumstances, it's especially difficult these days for many teachers as a result of the current public-education policy culture in the United States (and abroad). For a host of reasons (see Meier and Wood 2004 or Olsen and Sexton 2009 for details), many teachers in U.S. public schools find themselves working in contexts that require them to teach in the mostly didactic and test-driven ways I described in Chapters 3 and 4. Many public schools (especially underperforming ones that serve low-income communities and/or students of color) are being pressured to revert to antiquated, erroneous forms of knowledge delivery and standardized, assessment-based models of instruction. Many teachers currently find themselves working in districts and schools that have been pressured to operate in increasingly constrained and narrowed ways.

TEXTBOX 6.5   THREE COMMON COMPLAINTS ABOUT THE CONTEMPORARY TEACHING LANDSCAPE

- The *No Child Left Behind Act* has imposed unpleasant changes on teaching or exacerbated old problems, including standardization of instruction, adherence to purchased texts and teaching scripts, increased emphasis on high-stakes standardized tests for students, pressure to conform, and increased surveillance of teachers.
- The *recent economic woes* have made teaching more difficult owing to sapped budgets that have caused school overcrowding, cost-cutting "fixes," decreased resources overall, and uncertainty about future employment for many teachers and teaching-support professionals.
- *Social malaise and cynicism* on the part of youth (and many adults) have added to the already formidable challenges of inspiring students to do well and to do good. As a result of widespread corruption, divisive social battles, and a planet in crisis, many Americans have lost their faith in social programs, public institutions in general, collective compassion, and the possibility of thoughtful civic discussion.

※

Now more than ever it's important for thoughtful, dedicated, idealistic individuals to enter teaching.

Dozens, if not hundreds, of researchers and educators have written about the challenges, flaws, and concerns associated with teaching in the current policy climate. (To learn more about No Child Left Behind, for example, see Glickman 2004; McDermott 2007; McGuinn 2006; Popham 2005; Sleeter 2007; and U.S. Department of Education n.d.) One concern of mine is that the current education climate may discourage idealistic, creative, committed people from becoming teachers. But now more than ever it's important for thoughtful, dedicated, idealistic individuals to enter teaching. The profession needs well-prepared, self-reflective iconoclasts who will teach well and demonstrate that teaching does not need to be a rote profession of accepting mandates, delivering prepackaged teaching scripts, and adhering lockstep to some fill-in-the-bubble future for ourselves and our students. I also hope that those teachers already in the profession will remain and that they will speak out for the kinds of student-centered, constructivist, democratic teaching principles and methods that they have found to make a positive difference in the lives of students.

None of this is to say that accountability, assessment, and some standardization aren't desperately needed in education. They are. Like any profession, especially one serving children, teaching should be continually scrutinized and systematically reviewed for quality control. A teacher is only as good as the academic gains and personal growth demonstrated by his or her students. However, there's enormous debate on what we're educating students for, what achievement actually looks like, and how to accurately measure the kinds of personal growth we want our schools to support. Standardized tests mostly capture factual recall, predictable analysis, and academic facets of learning. That leaves out creative and independent reasoning, moral and social development, and diverse ways of thinking about (and solving) the dilemmas of contemporary life. Teaching is complicated partly because there's no consensus on what education is for.

PURPOSES OF EDUCATION

Any discussion of teaching and learning assessment should necessarily draw us back to contemplate the foundational question, *What's the purpose of education?* Since the current policy culture frequently has educators "teaching to the test," we must be clear on what the test is because, in a top-down testing policy culture, that is what will shape what happens in schools and classrooms. Are correct dates, formulas, and word definitions the test? Or is the test about interpreting and analyzing complex bodies of information for oneself? Is the test about one's ability to learn and articulate the dominant beliefs of our society? Or could the test perhaps be something more collective or cooperative instead—such as an informed and caring citizenry or a workforce full of productive, self-actualized human beings?

Educational historian David Labaree (1997) argued that much of the complexity in modern schools derives from the fact that there is no single answer for the question *What's education for?* There are three, and each answer sets in motion a different—and sometimes competing—conception of how education should be organized and what teachers ought to do. One purpose of education that Labaree put forward was *democratic equity*: schools teach the next generation of citizens to accept, perpetuate, and improve on the values for which our nation stands.

A second purpose, according to Labaree, is *social efficiency*: schools prepare workers so the United States can

---

TEXTBOX 6.6

What do *you* believe is the primary purpose of education? Why do you believe this? How does this belief of yours shape your students' opportunities?

compete successfully in the global economy. Laboree's third purpose for education is *social mobility*: schools provide children the means and opportunities to achieve their own individual success in the world.

These three purposes of education don't always align. For example, if you believe that education's primary purpose is to prepare workers to compete in the global economy, in your teaching you may sacrifice some dimensions of democratic equity (such as cooperative learning, critical examinations of capitalism, or candid lessons about ethics). Or if you believe individual social mobility is the goal of schooling, you may be less interested in broad notions of equity that you don't believe directly benefit the particular students in front of you. In short, how groups in society define education shapes how our schools are organized. And, similarly, how you define education has a lot to do with how you will teach. Therefore, I hope you will continually and critically plumb the depths of your educational beliefs.

These broad questions about education's fundamental purposes bring us back to a quotation presented in Chapter 1: David Cohen and Barbara Neufield (1981) writing that schooling is a grand theater in which any society plays out its cultural conflicts. I used to believe that once we fixed education, society would follow. Then, after a few years in the teaching profession, I came to believe that it was the other way around: schools will improve only when we get our society in order. But now, having worked in education for close to twenty years, I realize it's actually an ongoing tension in which each side—schools and society—affects the other, and change comes by way of the complex, active relationship between them. Education can push society to improve even at the same time that society is pushing education to improve. That's why self-reflective, excellent teachers are such an important part of our society.

However, any look at the current policy climate in education reminds us that individual teachers, no matter how talented and committed they are, are constrained by the educational institutions in which they work. How schools are organized, funding equations and resource allocations, mandated curricula, and the procedures for hiring and supporting teachers are all powerful structural and policy characteristics that affect who teaches, where they teach, and how they are permitted to conduct their work. In addition, education historians call our attention to the many unwritten, taken-for-granted ways in which the prior century (and the one before it) still organizes what happens in schools. Putting desks in rows with the teacher up front, bounding knowledge by traditional subject-matter labels such as "language arts" or "biology," and breaking up the school day with periods and bells are just a few examples of what researchers David Tyack and Larry Cuban (1995) called "the grammar of schooling." With that term they meant to make visible the system of built-in rules that seem to have lasted forever and that subtly shape what teachers and students do.

Institutional and historical influences on teachers should be examined and attended to, but they should not be considered as imprisoning teachers. Of course, teachers cannot be held responsible for all the failings of education. Teachers sometimes have to work harder than they should have to in order to teach well. And the profession would benefit from thousands of additional people capable of serving as innovative administrators, policymakers, and educational advocates. Yet teachers, although they may not be unfettered in their abilities and effects, still occupy the most important position in education.

Education stakeholders such as politicians, community groups, researchers, professors, and policymakers are significant parts of school reform, but it's teachers who are at the center of children's schooling. Teachers are not passive, empty, interchangeable automatons but active, unique individuals, often well prepared, with great influence over how student learning unfolds. It's likely that you chose teaching at least partly because you want to

**Cross-Reference
See Book 4.**

make a difference: you want to support young people to become the best they can be and improve the world in the process.

WHERE DO WE GO FROM HERE?

So, today's educational climate has made teaching both particularly difficult and more important than ever. This means that your ability to be an excellent educator is pivotal. How will you do so even in the current, sometimes unaccommodating, policy culture? As a way of bringing this book to a close, I offer five recommendations.

Analyze and Maximize Your Teacher Identity

Treat your teacher identity as the primary unit of analysis of your teacher development. Your teacher identity is the place where all your personal and professional, social and individual, past and present experiences combine into a tangle of professional beliefs, values, practices, and predictions for your teaching work. It's the whole ball of wax, so to speak. This makes it a useful topic for your teacher reflection, your professional development, your collegial conversations, and your ways of leveraging change in the kind of educator you are becoming. Engage in the strategies and activities of this book by yourself and with others in order to excavate, interrogate, and modify the many parts of your professional self.

Choose Your School Site Wisely

Working in a school that doesn't fit your teacher identity will cause neither you nor your students to succeed. It may even burn you out or push you out of the profession. Instead, you should make the effort required to find and join a school where the predominant practices, the majority of the people, and the preferred philosophies of education match your professional talents and goals. I've seen teachers who flourish in one school and feel miserable in another. A teacher-identity focus will help you to "know thyself," and thus will help you choose a school that will encourage you to flower rather than wither.

Cross-Reference
See Book 3.

This is not to suggest, however, that you should avoid people who are different from you, or perspectives that are not exactly like your own, or educational settings that use methods you are not used to. Diversity is a valuable part of any healthy educational context. Embracing different and new ideas will develop your teacher identity and improve your teaching. Students benefit from different teachers and from exposure to a heterodoxy of perspectives. So do teachers. I suggest you identify specific facets of "fit" that require a close match in order for you to thrive (for example, a like-minded approach to classroom organization and school discipline, or a shared view of the purposes of education), the dimensions in which you will actively seek diversity (perhaps faculty political viewpoints and cultural backgrounds), and issues that do not matter that much to you (for example, commute time or grade-level assignment).

Career coaches sometimes recommend that people thinking about their careers make a point of remembering wonderful, powerful events of their past and identify what they were doing at the time—and why it seemed so satisfying. "If you write those things down," one career counselor says, "there's a good chance you'll find the thread tying them together. And that will tell you a lot [about what kind of work to pursue]."[2] Teachers contemplating their own career choices and where to teach should do the same: What has made me feel successful and satisfied? How can I best make a difference for students? What do I need in order to be successful?

Employ Teacher-Identity Strategies to Stay Positive and Satisfied in Your Work

It's been said that teaching is a long-term struggle sustained by hope. In my own research I've found again and again that most teachers have a somewhat ambivalent relationship to their chosen profession. Teaching can be wonderfully rewarding and life-affirming, and it offers decent pay as well as work that allows you to grow and find your own challenges. But it can also be impossibly difficult, thankless, and energy-draining. You must not neglect the personal sides of your life. Since your personal self is implicated in your professional self, it follows that your professional self will be strengthened by care for your personal self. Be vigilant and dedicated as a teacher, but don't overdo it—you should plan on a long and productive career in education, not a short, fiery burst that ends in burnout.

Find support, solace, and happiness in your work and in your life wherever you can. Work collaboratively with others and find teacher-identity allies. Passionately pursue those professional development activities and educational projects that can reenergize you. Take on new educational roles in addition to teaching (but find ways to receive release-time or extra pay for them: your new roles should not come *on top of* an already full teaching assignment). Learning to teach takes commitment, patience, and a certain kind of faith in the future. It's not easy, but it's worth it.

Cross-Reference See Book 6.

View Yourself as Part of a Larger Team or Network of Educators

The kind of teacher-based, educational activism that goes above and beyond the classroom walls, and that this book calls out for, is hard work, and often emotionally taxing. Success is incremental—frequently of the two-steps-forward-one-step-backward variety. You don't want to feel like you're doing it alone, that you're a solitary voice in the wilderness. Instead, join like-minded groups of educators. If you can't find any, start your own. Encourage your teacher-education programs and mentorship groups to set up teacher support groups so that new teachers can stay connected to their peers, keep abreast of

Cross-Reference See Book 3, Chapter 3, for more on the importance of building professional networks.

current education research and practices, and benefit from the emotional and political support those systems provide.

To get back to the "birds of a feather" point from earlier in this chapter—the concern that people in life tend to surround themselves with like-minded folks—I believe that teachers should look for voices that do not merely reflect their own. As teachers navigate the tricky political issues in school and the events in their classrooms, they should seek out alternative viewpoints and experiences. Handling sensitive professional situations with a couple of like-minded peers might cause you to neglect the broader perspective that developing your teacher identity requires. Conversations with non-like-minded others can help build the kind of professional relationships that will lead to positive change. Again, balance is the key: like-minded colleagues can offer comfort and support, while diverse-thinking colleagues can offer growth and change. Seek out both types.

Always Work for Change

No matter how good a teacher you believe you are, or how well-performing your school is, there's always room for improvement. Continue to examine and develop your professional identity. After a few years in the profession, as you stabilize as a teacher, look for new challenges and begin to define your sphere of influence more widely.

Teachers have a responsibility first and foremost to be high-quality instructors and mentors to their students. But in order to be successful at that they may also need to eventually become professionally active outside the classroom. To do so requires becoming knowledgeable about school policy, education reform, and strategies for effecting social change. Once you become knowledgeable about aspects of education that are larger than (but no more important than) classroom instruction, you may wish to join with other educators to advocate for sensible school reform. As your competence and confidence as a teacher increase, so, too, should your motivation to take on issues of your whole school's climate and significant education matters in your district and state. Who's better positioned to speak for students and articulate smart ways to improve schooling than teachers? If you don't take this on, who will?

Develop your ability to argue persuasively for the kind of teaching you believe in. I have been present in staff meetings, school board hearings, and other forums where teachers have argued effectively for particular educational practices or teaching policy changes. The successful arguments are often those that are eloquent, articulated in terms of research and educational logic, and stated in terms of success for the students. Become knowledgeable about education reform, practice making arguments in public venues, and let listeners see your professionalism and your passion for supporting student success. I'm not suggesting that this is simple, or for everyone, and probably not always for beginning teachers (who have yet to demonstrate their own educational excellence). The new, idealist teacher who raises the torch in a faculty meeting of veterans could lose more than gain in that interaction. A school is not changed overnight, and neither are the broader influences that impact policy issues in education.

Instead, I suggest to new teachers that they read the lay of the land, look for low-hanging fruit, and remember that change is a long process. Be patient: find opportunities to make small differences, and then build on those efforts in the next arena. At first, become known in the school as a person with a passion who can unite a few others to create positive change. Larger leadership roles will follow as you produce successful outcomes. And always focus on what's best for students, their learning, and their school environment, because that's the type of activism that builds confidence and support at the administrative and policy levels of the school.

CONCLUSION

A healthy teacher identity is a complex, exciting thing to behold. It's long-lasting; its many parts work together (not against one another); it's the basis for successful, satisfying work with both children and adults; and it contributes to a successful, satisfying personal life. After these many pages on the topic, I don't really need to say it again, but I can't resist: your personal self and your teacher self work together in dozens of subtle, profound ways to produce the well-rounded, holistic, and continually changing assemblage that I call your teacher identity. Take care of it!

DISCUSSION QUESTIONS

1. What events and attitudes related to race, ethnicity, class, gender, sexuality, religion, language fluency, physical ability, and other cultural dimensions were dominant during your upbringing?

2. When did you first begin noticing issues of race, class, culture, and other dimensions? What were the circumstances? Who was involved? What do you think you took away from those early encounters? What, specifically, were the attitudes held by family, friends, and your community?

3. What aspects of your own views on race, culture, poverty, religion, and sexual orientation probably enter into your teaching? In what ways do they influence your teaching practices? Are you all right with that? Would the parents of these children be all right with that?

4. What are some social justice–related practices, conversations, and activities you would like to do with students in the classroom, but are reluctant to do? Why are you reluctant? What, specifically, do you think you need to learn about social-justice teaching in order to become better prepared and more comfortable doing such things with your own students?

FURTHER READING

Denner, J., and B. Guzman, eds. 2006. *Latina Girls: Voices of Adolescent Strength in the United States.* New York: New York University Press.

Leonardo, Z. 2004. "The Color of Supremacy: Beyond the Discourse of 'White Privilege.'" *Educational Philosophy and Theory* 36, no. 2: 137–152.

McIntosh, P. 1998. "White Privilege, Color, and Crime: A Personal Account." In C. R. Mann and M. Zatz, eds., *Images of Color, Images of Crime.* Los Angeles: Roxbury.

Pollock, M. 2005. *Colormute: Race Talk Dilemmas in an American School.* Princeton, NJ: Princeton University Press.

NOTES

1. In using the term *race, culture, and power,* I do not mean to exclude other significant social strata such as sexuality, religion, language, nationality, physical ability, or ethnicity, just to name a few. And readers should consider the multitude of cultural and social dimensions in play for their own teaching. But for reasons of succinctness and clarity I sometimes truncate the full list in this chapter.

2. These quoted remarks come from a magazine article about career choices ("Time Out," *New York*, August 1, 2009, 45).

APPENDIX

YOUR TEACHER
IDENTITY WORKSHEET

PART ONE

Use each prompt below to reflect on your relevant lived experiences and, on your own paper, provide brief summaries of the categories listed.

1. Think about and describe significant events, characteristics, aspects, and lessons of your *personal history* and *entry into teaching*.

    A. Family/home:

    B. Neighborhood(s) growing up:

    C. Friends and others in your life:

    D. K–8 schooling experience:

    E. High-school experience:

    F. College and university experience:

    G. Why did you decide to become a teacher?

    H. How did the people around you react to your career decision?

2. Thinking about what you have already written, identify and write down five or six of the larger *themes or aspects of your own personal history*. We might call these *life themes*. Examples might include "a strong commitment to equity and fairness in life," or "a constant desire to see the good in everyone," or "a nagging pessimism about the future."

My life themes are the following:

3. Now, reflect on and describe (in as much detail as you can) your *teacher-preparation program* and your *experience there*.

A. What were the dominant theories, attitudes, and professional characteristics of your teacher-preparation program (that is, your university teacher-education program or alternative teacher-preparation program[1])? Put another way, what kind of teacher does (or did) your preparation program want you to be?

B. How did your own incoming ideas and identity fit with your professional program? Was it mostly a confirming relationship, a disconfirming (or conflicting) relationship, or maybe a little of both?

C. Identify ways in which your personal history has overlapped and/or conflicted with the various characteristics of your teacher-preparation program and your experience there.

D. Return to the life themes you listed above, and consider how they (and other aspects of your personal history) may have shaped (or are currently shaping) your teacher-preparation experience. How do they interact with your own beginning teacher learning to influence the teacher you are becoming?

PART TWO

Consider the ways in which your personal history and your professional preparation have combined to make you into the teacher you are now.

1. Let's move to how these *life themes* you've identified, and their *connections to your teacher preparation*, may have become aspects of your *current teacher identity*. In other words, what influences from your personal history, mixed with your teacher-education experience, are active parts of your current teacher self?

   A. Ways that I conceptualize my subject matter as a teacher:

   B. Ways that I view and treat my students:

   C. The kinds of instructional practices I favor (and why):

   D. The kinds of instructional practices I reject (and why):

   E. My teaching purposes and how I define "success" for myself and students:

   F. My relationships with colleagues and administrators:

   G. My predictions for my future in education:

2. Now, to conclude, reflect on *aspects of your teacher identity that in fact you want to adjust or improve*. What are some things about your professional self that you now realize may derive from your personal history and that—in the light of day—you realize need adjusting?

   A. What are some aspects of your teaching or teacher identity that you wish to adjust or improve?

   B. Where do you suppose those identity characteristics of yours come from?

C. What will you do, concretely and purposefully, to alter or adjust those aspects of your teacher identity?

D. What will you look for, afterward, in order to know whether or not your intended changes have succeeded?

NOTE

1. By "alternative teacher-preparation program" I mean nonuniversity paths into teaching (for example, Teach for America, a particular teacher internship program, emergency certification, or some other teacher entrance program).

REFERENCES

Allport, G. 1968. *The Person in Psychology*. Boston: Beacon Press.

Anderson, J., L. Reder, J. Greeno, and H. Simon. 2000. "Perspectives on Learning, Thinking and Activity." *Educational Researcher* 29, no. 4.

Anderson, L., and B. Olsen. 2006. "Investigating Early Career Urban Teachers' Perspectives on and Experiences in Professional Development." *Journal of Teacher Education* 57, no. 4: 359–377.

Ashton, P. T., and R. B. Webb. 1986. *Making a Difference: Teachers' Sense of Self-Efficacy and Student Achievement*. White Plains, NY: Longman.

Ayers, B. 2001. *To Teach: The Journey of a Teacher*. New York: Teachers College Press.

Bandura, A. 1982. "Self-Efficacy Mechanism in Human Agency." *American Psychologist* 37, no. 2: 122–147.

———. 1993. "Perceived Self-Efficacy in Cognitive Development and Functioning." *Educational Psychologist* 28, no. 2: 117–148.

———, ed. 1995. *Self-Efficacy in Changing Societies*. New York: Cambridge University Press.

Banks, J., and C. A. McGee Banks, eds. 2005. *Handbook of Research on Multicultural Education*, 2nd ed. San Francisco: Jossey-Bass.

Beijaard, D., P. C. Meijer, and N. Verloop. 2004. "Reconsidering Research on Teachers' Professional Identity." *Teaching and Teacher Education* 20: 107–128.

Belenky, M. F., B. Clinchy, N. Goldberger, and J. Tarulule. 1986. *Women's Ways of Knowing: The Development of Self, Voice, and Mind*. New York: Basic Books.

Bourdieu, P. 1991. *Language and Symbolic Power*. Cambridge, MA: Harvard University Press.

Bowles, S., and H. Gintis. 1975. *Schooling in Capitalist America*. New York: Basic Books.

Brookfield, S. 2006. *The Skillful Teacher*. San Francisco: Jossey-Bass.

Calderhead, J. 1988. "The Development of Knowledge Structures in Learning to Teach." In J. Calderhead, ed., *Teachers' Professional Learning*. Philadelphia: Falmer Press.

Chubbuck, S. M., and M. Zembylas. 2008. "The Emotional Ambivalence of Socially Just Teaching: A Case Study of a Novice Urban School Teacher." *American Educational Research Journal* 45, no. 2: 274–318.

Clark, C. M., and R. J. Yinger. 1979. "Teacher Thinking." In P. L. Peterson and H. J. Walberg, eds., *Research on Teaching*. Berkeley, CA: McCutchan.

Clifford, G., and J. Guthrie. 1988. *Ed School*. Chicago: University of Chicago Press.

Cobb, P. 1994. "Where Is the Mind? Constructivist and Sociocultural Perspectives on Mathematical Development." *Educational Researcher* 23, no. 7: 13–20.

Cobb, P., and J. Bowers. 1999. "Cognitive and Situated Learning Perspectives in Theory and Practice." *Educational Researcher* 28, no. 2.

Cochran-Smith, M., and S. Lytle. 1993. *Inside/Outside: Teacher Research and Knowledge*. New York: Teachers College Press.

Cochran-Smith, M., and K. Zeichner, eds. 2005. *Studying Teacher Education: The Report of the AERA Panel on Research and Teacher Education*. Mahwah, NJ: Lawrence Erlbaum Associates.

Cohen, D., and B. Neufield. 1981. "The Failure of High Schools and the Progress of Education." *Daedalus* 110 (Summer): 69–89.

Coles, R., and R. Testa, eds. 2002. *A Life in Medicine: A Literary Anthology*. New York: The New Press.

Constantine, J., D. Player, T. Silva, K. Hallgren, M. Grider, and J. Deke. 2009. *An Evaluation of Teachers Trained through Different Routes to Certification, Final Report* (NCEE 2009-4043). Washington, DC: National Center for Education Evaluation and Regional Assistance, Institute of Education Sciences, U.S. Department of Education.

Csikszentmihalyi, M. 2008. *Flow: The Psychology of Optimal Experience*. New York: HarperPerennial Modern Classics.

Cuban, L. 1993. *How Teachers Taught: Constancy and Change in American Classrooms*. New York: Teachers College Press.

Darder, A. M. Boldodano, and R. Torres. 2003. *The Critical Pedagogy Reader*. New York: RoutledgeFalmer.

Darling–Hammond, L., A. Wise, and S. Klein. 1995. *A License to Teach: Building a Profession for Twenty-First Century Schools*. Boulder: Westview Press.

Delpit, L. 1995. *Other People's Children: Cultural Conflict in the Classroom*. New York: The New Press.

Denner, J., and B. Guzman, eds. 2006. *Latina Girls: Voices of Adolescent Strength in the United States*. New York: New York University Press.

Dewey, J. 1904. "The Relation of Theory to Practice in the Education of Teachers." In C. McMurry, ed., *The Third Yearbook of the National Society for the Scientific Study of Education*. Chicago: University of Chicago Press.

———. 1916. *Democracy and Education*. New York: The Free Press.

———. 1933. *How We Think: A Restatement of the Relation of Reflective Thinking to the Educative Process*. New York: D. C. Heath.

Feiman-Nemser, S. 1990. "Teacher Education: Structural and Conceptual Alternatives." In W. R. Houston, ed., *Handbook of Research on Teacher Education*. New York: Macmillan.

Feiman-Nemser, S., and M. Buchmann. 1985. "Pitfalls of Experience in Teacher Preparation." *Teachers College Record* 87, no. 1: 53–65.

Fosnot, C., ed. 2005. *Constructivism*. New York: Teachers College Press.

Foucault, M. 1970. *The Order of Things*. Translated by A. M. Sheridan Smith. New York: Vintage Books.

———. 1977. *Discipline and Punish: The Birth of the Prison*. Translated by Alan Sheridan. New York: Pantheon.

Freedman, S. W., E. R. Simons, and J. S. Kalnin. 1999. *Inside City Schools: Investigating Literacy in Multicultural Classrooms*. New York: Teachers College Press.

Freire, P. 1970. *Pedagogy of the Oppressed*. Translated by M. B. Ramos. New York: Continuum.

———. 1985. *Politics of Education: Culture, Power, and Liberation*. Translated by Donaldo Macedo. South Hadley, MA: Bergin and Garvey.

Fuller, F., and O. Bown. 1975. "Becoming a Teacher." In K. Ryan, ed., *Teacher Education*, 74th yearbook of the National Society for the Study of Education, Part II. Chicago: University of Chicago Press.

Gardner, H. 1991. *The Unschooled Mind: How Children Think and How Schools Should Teach*. New York: Basic Books.

Gaughan, J. 2001. *Reinventing English: Teaching in the Contact Zone*. Portsmouth, NH: Boynton-Cook.

Gladwell, M. 2008. "Most Likely to Succeed." *New Yorker*, December 15, 2008.

Glickman, C., ed. 2004. *Letters to the Next President: What We Can Do about the Real Crisis in Public Education*. New York: Teachers College Press.

Gmelch, W. H. 1983. "Stress for Success: How to Optimize Your Performance." *Theory into Practice* 22, no. 1: 7–14.

Gold, Y. 1993. *Teachers Managing Stress and Preventing Burnout: The Professional Health Solution*. Philadelphia: Falmer.

Gonzalez, N., L. Moll, and C. Amanti. 2005. *Funds of Knowledge: Theorizing Practices in Households, Communities, and Classrooms.* Mahwah, NJ: Lawrence Erlbaum Associates.

Good, T. L., B. J. Biddle, and J. E. Brophy. 1975. *Teachers Make a Difference.* New York: Holt, Rinehart and Winston.

Grossman, P. 1990. *The Making of a Teacher: Teacher Knowledge and Teacher Education.* New York: Teachers College Press.

Grossman, P., C. Compton, D. Igra, M. Ronfeldt, E. Shahan, and P. Williamson. 2009. "Teaching Practice: A Cross-Professional Perspective." *Teachers College Record* 111, no. 9.

Grumet, M. R. 1994. "Reading the Relations of Teaching." *Psychoanalytic Psychology* 11: 253–263.

Haberman, M. 1990. "Urban Teachers Who Quit: Why They Leave and What They Do." *Urban Education* 25, no. 3: 297–303.

Hamachek, D. 1999. "Effective Teachers: What They Do, How They Do It, and the Importance of Self-Knowledge." In R. Lipka and T. Brinthaupt, eds., *The Role of Self in Teacher Development.* Albany: State University of New York Press.

Hargreaves, A. 1995. *Changing Teachers, Changing Times: Teachers' Work and Culture in the Postmodern Age.* London: Cassell.

———. 1998. "The Emotional Practice of Teaching." *Teaching and Teacher Education* 14, no. 8: 835–854.

hooks, b. 1981. *Ain't I a Woman? Black Women and Feminism.* Boston: South End Press.

———. 1994. *Teaching to Transgress.* New York: Routledge.

Huberman, M. 1993. *The Lives of Teachers.* Translated by J. Neufeld. New York: Teachers College Press.

Igoa, C. 1995. *The Inner World of the Immigrant Child.* Mahwah, NJ: Lawrence Earlbaum Associates.

Jackson, P. 1986. *The Practice of Teaching.* New York: Teachers College Press.

Kliebard, H. 1995. *The Struggle for the American Curriculum.* New York: Routledge.

Kozol, J. 1991. *Savage Inequalities: Children in America's Schools.* New York: HarperPerennial.

Krashen, S. 1987. *Principles and Practice in Second Language Acquisition.* Boston: Prentice-Hall International.

Labaree, D. F. 1997. "Public Goods, Private Goods: The American Struggle over Educational Goals." *American Educational Research Journal* 34.

Ladson Billings, Gloria. 1994. *The Dreamkeepers: Successful Teachers of African American Children.* San Francisco: Jossey-Bass.

Lakoff, G., and M. Turner. 1989. *More Than Cool Reason: A Field Guide to Poetic Metaphor*. Chicago: University of Chicago Press.

Lave, J. 1988. *Cognition in Practice: Mind, Mathematics, and Culture in Everyday Life*. Cambridge: Cambridge University Press.

Lave, J., and E. Wenger. 1991. *Situated Learning*. Cambridge: Cambridge University Press.

Leonardo, Z. 2004. "The Color of Supremacy: Beyond the Discourse of 'White Privilege.'" *Educational Philosophy and Theory* 36, no. 2: 137–152.

Lieberman, A., and L. Miller. 2008. *Teachers in Professional Communities: Improving Teaching and Learning*. New York: Teachers College Press.

Lieberman, A., and D. Wood. 2006. *Inside the National Writing Project: Connecting Network Learning and Classroom Teaching*. New York: Teachers College Press.

Lipka, R., and T. Brinthaupt, eds. 1999. *The Role of Self in Teacher Development*. Albany: State University of New York Press.

Little, J. W. 1996. "The Emotional Contours and Career Trajectories of (Disappointed) Reform Enthusiasts." *Cambridge Journal of Education* 26, no. 3: 345–359.

Lortie, D. 1975. *Schoolteacher: A Sociological Study*. Chicago: University of Chicago Press.

Mamet, D. 2009. "We Can't Stop Talking about Race in America." *New York Times*, September 13, 2009.

Mann, H. 1868. *The Eclectic Magazine* 7 (January–June).

McDermott, K. 2007. "'Expanding the Moral Community' or 'Blaming the Victim'? The Politics of State Educational Accountability Policy." *American Educational Research Journal* 44, no. 1: 77–111.

McGuinn, P. 2006. *No Child Left Behind and the Transformation of Federal Education Policy, 1965–2006*. Lawrence: University Press of Kansas.

McIntosh, P. 1998. "White Privilege, Color, and Crime: A Personal Account." In C. R. Mann and M. Zatz, eds., *Images of Color, Images of Crime*. Los Angeles: Roxbury.

McLaren, P., and J. Kincheloe, eds. 2007. *Critical Pedagogy: Where Are We Now?* New York: Peter Lang.

Meier, D., and G. Wood. 2004. *Many Children Left Behind: How the No Child Left Behind Act Is Damaging Our Children and Our Schools*. Boston: Beacon Press.

Michie, G. 1999. *Holler If You Hear Me: The Education of a Teacher and His Students*. New York: Teachers College Press.

Moore Johnson, S., and the Project on the Next Generation of Teachers. 2004. *Finders and Keepers: Helping New Teachers Survive and Thrive in Our Schools*. San Francisco: Jossey-Bass.

Moyers, B. 1990. *A World of Ideas II*. New York: Doubleday.

Muir, J. 1988 [1911]. *My First Summer in the Sierra*. San Francisco: Sierra Club Books.

Murphy, M. 1990. *Blackboard Unions: The AFT and the NEA, 1900–1980*. Ithaca, NY: Cornell University Press.

Noddings, N. 2003. *Caring: A Feminine Approach to Ethics and Moral Education*, 2nd ed. Berkeley: University of California Press.

Oakes, J., and M. Lipton. 2006. *Teaching to Change the World*. Boston: McGraw Hill.

Olsen, B. 2008a. *Teaching What They Learn, Learning What They Live: How Teachers' Personal Histories Shape Their Professional Development*. Boulder: Paradigm Publishers.

———. 2008b. "How Reasons for Entry into the Profession Illuminate Teacher Identity Development." *Teacher Education Quarterly* 35, no. 3: 23–32.

———. 2010. "I Am Large, I Contain Multitudes": Teacher Identity as Useful Frame for Research, Practice, and Diversity in Teacher Education." In A. Ball and C. Tyson, eds., *The American Educational Research Association Handbook on Studying Diversity in Teacher Education*. Lanham, MD: Rowman and Littlefield.

Olsen, B., and D. Sexton. 2008. "Threat Rigidity, School Reform, and How Teachers View Their Work inside Current Educational Contexts." *American Educational Research Journal* 46, no. 1: 9–44.

Palmer, P. 1998. *The Courage to Teach: Exploring the Inner Landscape of a Teacher's Life*. San Francisco: Jossey-Bass.

Pettinger, P. 1998. *Bill Evans: How My Heart Sings*. New Haven, CT: Yale University Press.

Pollock, M. 2005. *Colormute: Race Talk Dilemmas in an American School*. Princeton, NJ: Princeton University Press.

Popham, J. 2005. *America's "Failing" Schools: How Parents and Teachers Can Cope with No Child Left Behind*. New York: Routledge.

Popkewitz, T., and M. Brennan, eds. 1998. *Foucault's Challenge: Discourse, Knowledge, and Power in Education*. New York: Teachers College Press.

Quartz, Karen Hunter, Brad Olsen, Lauren Anderson, and Kimberly Barraza Lyons. *Making a Difference: Developing Meaningful Careers in Education*. Teachers Toolkit Series (in this set). Boulder: Paradigm.

Rich, A. 1978/1993. "Compulsory Heterosexuality and Lesbian Existence." In H. Abelove, D. M. Halperin, and M. A. Barale, eds., *The Lesbian and Gay Reader*. New York: Routledge.

Rogers, C. 1969. *The Freedom to Learn*. Columbus, OH: Merrill.

Rust, F. 1994. "The First Year of Teaching: It's Not What They Expected." *Teaching and Teacher Education* 10, no. 2: 205–217.

Shavelson, R. J., and P. Stern. 1981. "Research on Teachers' Pedagogical Thoughts, Judgments, Decisions and Behaviors." *Review of Education Research* 51: 455–498.

Shor, I. 1987. *Critical Teaching and Everyday Life*. Chicago: University of Chicago Press.

Shulman, L. 1986. "Those Who Understand: Knowledge Growth in Teaching." *Educational Researcher* 15, no. 2: 4–14.

Sleeter, C. 2005. *Un-standardizing Curriculum: Multicultural Teaching in the Standards-Based Classroom*. New York: Teachers College Press.

———. 2007. *Facing Accountability in Education*. New York: Teachers College Press.

Stegner, W. 1990. *The Spectator Bird*. New York: Penguin.

Sutton, R., and K. Wheatley. 2003. "Teachers' Emotions and Teaching: A Review of the Literature and Directions for Future Research." *Educational Psychology Review* 15, no. 4: 327–358.

Tatum, B. 1997. *Why Are All the Black Kids Sitting Together in the Cafeteria? And Other Conversations about Race*. New York: Basic Books.

Tremmel, R. 1993. "Zen and the Art of Reflective Process in Teacher Education." *Harvard Educational Review* 63, no. 4: 434–458.

Tyack, D., and L. Cuban. 1995. *Tinkering toward Utopia: A Century of Public School Reform*. New York: Teachers College Press.

U.S. Department of Education. (n.d.). "No Child Left Behind Information Centers." Retrieved May 22, 2008, from www.ed.gov/nclb.

White, E. B. 1974 [1945]. *Stuart Little*. Illustrations by Garth Williams. New York: HarperCollins.

Wideen, M., J. Mayer-Smith, and B. Moon. 1998. "A Critical Analysis of the Research on Learning to Teach: Making the Case for an Ecological Perspective on Inquiry." *Review of Educational Research* 68, no. 2: 130–178.

Will, G. 2006. "Ed Schools versus Education: Prospective Teachers Are Expected to Have the Correct 'Disposition,' Proof of Which Is Espousing 'Progressive' Political Beliefs." *Newsweek*, January 16, 2006.

Willis, P. 1981. *Learning to Labour: How Working Class Kids Get Working Class Jobs*. New York: Columbia University Press.

Wilson, T. 2004. *Strangers to Ourselves: Discovering the Adaptive Unconscious*. Cambridge: Harvard University Press.

Wink, J. 2004. *Critical Pedagogy: Notes from the Real World*. Boston: Allyn and Bacon.

Woolfolk, A. E., and W. K. Hoy. 1990. "Prospective Teachers' Sense of Self-Efficacy and Belief about Control." *Journal of Educational Psychology* 82: 81–91.

Zehm, S., and J. Kottler. 1993. *On Being a Teacher: The Human Dimension.* Newbury Park, CA: Corwin Press.

Zeichner, K., and B. Tabachnick. 1981. "Are the Effects of Teacher Education Washed Out by School Experience?" *Journal of Teacher Education* 32, no. 3: 7–11.

INDEX

ABOUT THE AUTHOR

Brad Olsen is Associate Professor of Education at the University of California, Santa Cruz. His research focuses primarily on teachers, teaching, and teacher education.

Dr. Olsen previously worked as a high school English teacher, school administrator, and teacher educator. He is the author of *Teaching What They Learn, Learning What They Live: How Teachers' Personal Histories Shape Their Professional Development* (Paradigm Publishers 2008).